The Cambridge Introduction to
William Faulkner

Known for his distinctive voice and his evocative depictions of life in the American South, Nobel laureate William Faulkner is recognized as one of the most important authors of the twentieth century. This introductory book provides students and readers of Faulkner with a clear overview of his life and work. His nineteen novels, including *The Sound and the Fury*, *As I Lay Dying*, *Absalom, Absalom!*, and *Go Down, Moses*, are discussed in detail, as are his major short stories and nonfiction. Focused on the works themselves, but also providing useful information about their critical reception, this *Introduction* is an accessible guide to Faulkner's challenging and complex oeuvre.

Theresa M. Towner is Professor of Literary Studies at the University of Texas at Dallas.

Cambridge Introductions to Literature

This series is designed to introduce students to key topics and authors. Accessible and lively, these introductions will also appeal to readers who want to broaden their understanding of the books and authors they enjoy.

- Ideal for students, teachers, and lecturers
- Concise, yet packed with essential information
- Key suggestions for further reading

Titles in this series:

The Cambridge Introduction to
William Faulkner

THERESA M. TOWNER

University of Texas at Dallas

CAMBRIDGE
UNIVERSITY PRESS

CAMBRIDGE UNIVERSITY PRESS
Cambridge, New York, Melbourne, Madrid, Cape Town, Singapore, São Paulo

Cambridge University Press
The Edinburgh Building, Cambridge CB2 8RU, UK

Published in the United States of America by Cambridge University Press, New York

www.cambridge.org
Information on this title: www.cambridge.org/9780521671552

First published 2008

Printed in the United Kingdom at the University Press, Cambridge

A catalogue record for this publication is available from the British Library

ISBN 978-0-521-85546-4 hardback
ISBN 978-0-521-67155-2 paperback

For Alison Leslie Sloan
– my girl

Contents

Abbreviations

Quotations will be cited parenthetically in the text by page number.

Blotner   Blotner, Joseph. *Faulkner: A Biography*, one-volume edition. New York: Random House, 1984.

SL   —, ed. *Selected Letters of William Faulkner*. New York: Vintage, 1978.

FCF   Cowley, Malcolm. *The Faulkner-Cowley File: Letters and Memories, 1944–1962*. New York: Viking, 1966; Penguin, 1978.

FIU   Gwynn, Frederick L. and Joseph L. Blotner, eds. *Faulkner in the University*. 1959. Charlottesville and London: University Press of Virginia, 1995.

ESPL   Meriwether, James B., ed. *William Faulkner: Essays, Speeches, and Public Letters*, updated edition. New York: Modern Library, 2004.

LIG   and Michael Millgate, eds. *Lion in the Garden: Interviews with William Faulkner, 1926–1962*. Lincoln and London: University of Nebraska Press, 1968; Bison Books, 1980.

Williamson   Williamson, Joel. *William Faulkner and Southern History*. Oxford: Oxford University Press, 1993.

Preface

The Mississippi-born, Nobel Prize-winning writer William Faulkner gave the world Yoknapatawpha County. He joined the Canadian Royal Air Force in the Great War and learned to fly but never saw action; he lived in Oxford, Mississippi, for nearly his whole life and once turned down an invitation to an artists' dinner from the Kennedy White House because he said it was too far to go to eat with strangers. He rode to the fox hounds in Charlottesville, Virginia, in his later years and had his portrait made in formal riding clothes, yet he was just as likely to pose for photographs in his tattered khakis and nearly ruined Harris tweed jacket. To say he cherished his privacy is to understate the case radically: he once wrote that "it is my ambition to be, as a private individual, abolished and voided from history . . . in the same sentence is my obit and epitaph too, shall be them both: He made the books and he died."

He has now done both those things – made the books and died – and more than forty years after his passing, he remains widely read, discussed, assigned, analyzed, and invoked. Every major school of criticism has been applied to his most famous novels; every major anthology of American and world literature includes his work. Most of the published commentary on Faulkner is written by and aimed at an academic and scholarly audience, yet most of Faulkner's new readers find him because teachers make students read his work in a variety of contexts and then take on the task of "explaining" what it means in class. Even Oprah Winfrey's Book Club consulted specialists for help. Yet such help, either printed or on the internet, often obscures understanding because of the uneven quality (and varying degrees of accuracy) in such a crowded field of study. That study tends to remain categorized by type – biography, textual analysis, influence study, historiography, and so forth. Because *The Cambridge Introduction to William Faulkner* treats Faulkner's life and work as well as their contexts and critical reception, this volume can serve as a reader's first stop in Faulkner criticism, as a companion reader of his texts more than the latest word in scholarship.

Readers may use this book either by reading it from beginning to end or by consulting sections of interest, including those devoted to individual texts.

Owing to space constraints I have not cited the original source of every idea herein but have instead relied on the published criticism to address what seem like the most common questions for a beginning reader to have. And whether one is a high school student, a curious adult reader, an undergraduate, or a senior citizen, when we begin to read Faulkner we all begin together – in confusion. But like Dante on his way through Inferno or Pilgrim on his Progress, we can come through it.

Let's begin.

Theresa M. Towner
University of Texas at Dallas

Chapter 1

Life

William Cuthbert Falkner was born late at night on September 25, 1897, and died early in the morning of July 6, 1962; were we to honor his wishes on the matter of his biography, we would not inquire into it any further than that. He was a quiet and intensely private man who once observed that "it is my ambition to be, as a private individual, abolished and voided from history"; "in the same sentence is my obit and epitaph too, shall be them both: He made the books and he died" (*FCF* 126). In his fiction, subconsciously and on purpose, Faulkner used the materials of his life in very subtle, often tertiary ways, and more than one biographer has gone terribly astray while trying to use the life to explain his work or the work to explain his life. Another problem in writing Faulkner's biography is raised by the fact that he was first and foremost a *fiction* writer. When asked a question about his private life, he was just as likely to make something up as he was when he sat at his typewriter at home inventing characters and plots. Early in his career, for example, he wrote to an editor who had asked for biographical information that he was "Born male and single at early age in Mississippi. Quit school after five years in seventh grade. Got job in Grandfather's bank and learned medicinal value of his liquor. Grandfather thought janitor did it. Hard on janitor" (*SL* 47). Yet Faulkner had a very interesting life, and we have a full record of it, and readers are understandably curious about the man who made the books and died. He came from a family with origins in Scotland who emigrated to the Carolinas. In about 1842 a man named William Clark Falkner walked from Missouri to Pontotoc, Mississippi, in search of an uncle by marriage, and thus did William Cuthbert Faulkner's great-grandfather settle in the state that would become as synonymous with a writer as Stratford-upon-Avon is with Shakespeare.

The first William Falkner married twice, fathered nine children, fought and commanded troops in the first part of the Civil War and ran blockades in the latter part, sired a "shadow family" with a former slave, made money in land speculation during Reconstruction, founded a railroad, and died of a gunshot fired by a former business partner with whom he had been feuding. Two things about him seem to have stuck in his famous great-grandson's imagination.

First, he was successful as an author as well as a man of action. His romantic novel *The White Rose of Memphis* (1881) appeared in thirty-five editions and sold 160,000 copies; his travel memoir *Rapid Ramblings in Europe* appeared after he took his daughter on vacation in 1883. Second, he made the family name both famous and infamous (Williamson 55–6). He was "a considerable figure in his time and provincial milieu," and in writing fiction the younger William both followed his lead and did him one better, changing the family name in the process: "Maybe when I began to write," he said, "I was secretly ambitious and did not want to ride on grandfather's coat-tails, and so accepted the 'u,' was glad of such an easy way to strike out for myself" (*SL* 211–12).

By all accounts the William Cuthbert Falkner born in 1897 to Maud and Murry Falkner in New Albany, Mississippi, had a happy boyhood. In 1902 the family moved to Oxford, Mississippi, where Murry worked first as a street construction supervisor and then as the owner of a livery stable, and a fourth son was born to them. Maud's mother, Leila, whom the boys called "Damuddy," moved in with the family, and from her and Maud William learned to draw, to appreciate music and the arts, and to read. During these years, William "gained an intimate knowledge of the Bible" (Williamson 145), a knowledge that would emerge time and again in his fiction, as would certain events of his early youth, like the death of his maternal grandmother. The family was joined in 1902 by Caroline Barr, the black woman born in slavery whom the Falkner children called "Mammy Callie" and who would help to raise them. Two doors away from their home in Oxford lived Lida Estelle Oldham, seven months older than William. In 1903 Estelle called the family maid's attention to that young gentleman: "See that boy, Nolia? The one in front? – the one riding the pony by himself? That's the one I'm going to marry" (Williamson 149). (Twenty-six years, one ex-husband, and two children later, she did.) As children in Oxford, William and his three younger brothers rode their ponies, learned to hunt and fish, and once even built and attempted to fly an airplane, with Billy as chief engineer and pilot (Blotner 34–5). All the boys listened to the stories told by their paternal grandfather, John Wesley Thompson Falkner, and by Callie Barr and other black retainers associated with the family; some of these, including chauffeur Chess Carothers and the blacksmith on his grandfather's farm, became prototypes of certain characters in his fiction (Blotner 31).

As he approached his teens, Billy Falkner began to develop a romantic interest in Estelle Oldham that was nurtured by their mutual love of poetry. He had always told stories and drawn pictures, and he brought Estelle poems that he thought she might like, including some he had written. He noticed that Estelle noticed him when he dressed well, and he developed a lifelong love of fine clothes and, as we shall see, of costumes and disguises. Undeniably a beauty, with dark hair and eyes and a vivacity made for the dances and music of America in the 'Teens, Estelle attracted handsome men. One of these, Cornell Franklin, gained the approval of her parents – an approval that the quiet, shy Billy did not have, primarily because of his poor earning potential and the higher social status of her family. They talked of but did not attempt elopement. Pressure from her parents increased; the marriage to Franklin was inevitable. Billy did not wait to see Estelle marry Franklin. Instead, he tried to enlist in pilot training for service in the Great War; his application was rejected, probably because he was too short.

In order to help his miserable friend, Oxford native and Yale student Phil Stone invited Billy to New Haven. A mutual friend had introduced them in the summer of 1914, saying that Billy wrote poems but did not know anyone who could help him figure out what to do with them (Blotner 44). Stone began to direct Billy's already avid reading, which came to include everything from Augustus Baldwin Longstreet, the humorist of the Old Southwest, to Sophocles, Plato, and Algernon Charles Swinburne. The invitation to New Haven came because Stone feared that Billy and Estelle would elope after all; he believed that marriage would ruin Billy's future as a writer, and Stone had been encouraging and directing that future for four very intense years of friendship and mentoring. To New Haven Billy went, and there, in consultation with Stone and his friends, a plan was hatched for him to enlist in the Canadian Royal Air Force for training that would eventually post him at the Western Front of the war in Europe. Such enlistment required massive deception on Billy's part: he started by changing the spelling of his last name to "Faulkner," learning and affecting a British accent, claiming an earlier birthday, and listing his hometown as Middlesex, England. He got in. The Armistice was signed while he was still in flight school in Toronto. His younger brother Jack served with the Marines in some of the war's most ferocious battles, but the most danger Billy saw in the war was the influenza epidemic of 1918 when it came through Toronto.

Bill Faulkner spent his discharge pay on the full dress uniform of an RAF pilot, including the chest-crossing Sam Browne belt and a cane. He came back to Oxford with a limp, claiming to have flown his airplane (while drunk) upside down through a hangar, which had resulted in the limp and a metal plate in his head. The disaffected RAF pilot was the first and arguably the flashiest of many personae that he would adopt throughout his lifetime. In Virginia near the end of his life, for instance, he wore the red coats and silks of the fox hunting club he frequented; he posed with airplanes and automobiles to suggest the figure of the man of motion; he let the camera capture him bearded and in an overcoat as a bohemian in Paris's Luxembourg Gardens. He was not always the dandy; he had a hick image that he put on to keep intellectuals and literary types at a distance, and he appeared in torn khakis and worn tweed jackets in photographs taken in every decade of his life. When he returned to Oxford after the Armistice, the townspeople saw the RAF uniform and the studied mannerisms and no visible means of financial support and consequently began to call him "Count No Account," or "Count No 'Count" for short. Even after he entered the University of Mississippi as a special student, the name stuck. For the next few years, he worked at odd jobs, the most famous of which was a three-year stint as postmaster at the university branch of the Post Office. He and his friends would play cards in the back while the public's mail went unattended or undelivered; he would read what mail he liked, primarily the literary magazines; he wrote much of the poetry for his first book there. In short, he was an awful postmaster, and when he was finally removed from the job, he said, "I reckon I'll be at the beck and call of folks with money all my life, but thank God I won't ever again have to be at the beck and call of every son of a bitch who's got two cents to buy a stamp" (Blotner 118). In an irony he would appreciate, the United States Post Office issued a William Faulkner stamp in 1987, so for a brief while he was at the beck and call of anyone with twenty-two cents to buy a stamp.

In the early 1920s Faulkner had published a few poems and pieces of literary criticism; in 1924, after the publication of his first book, he set out for New Orleans. There he met the established American writer Sherwood Anderson, whose *Winesburg, Ohio* (1919) showed a new generation of writers new possibilities for the subjects and techniques of fiction. In particular, Anderson had revealed the claustrophobia and hopelessness of small-town modern America. He advised Faulkner to write about what he knew best: "You're a country boy; all you know is that little patch up there in Mississippi where you started from. But that's all right too. It's America too; pull it out, as little and unknown as it is, and the whole thing will collapse, like when you prize a brick out of a wall" (*ESPL* 7). Before he took that advice, however, Faulkner had written (and Anderson had helped him to publish) his first novel, *Soldiers' Pay* (1926), about the wounded generation of men and women that survived the Great War. He wrote that novel in New Orleans and set his second one there; *Mosquitoes* (1927) concerns a group of artists and artist-wannabes on a houseboat trip, and it includes a short self-portrait of Faulkner himself as an "awful sunburned and kind of shabby dressed" man who "said he was a liar by profession." The mention of his name generates this response: "'Faulkner?' the niece pondered in turn. 'Never heard of him,' she said at last, with finality."[1]

With his third novel, *Sartoris*, and his fourth, *The Sound and the Fury* (both published in 1929), the literary world heard of him, indeed. This fiction began an intensely productive period in Faulkner's writing life. The years between

1929 and 1942 saw the publication of eleven novels, two collections of short stories, about forty-five individual stories, and a collection of poetry. He made his living as a writer during the entirety of the Great Depression and was nearly always desperate for money. He wrote and sold short stories as fast as he could (which he called "boiling the pot" [*SL* 114]) because popular magazines with large revenues and budgets paid extremely well. The *Saturday Evening Post* and *American Mercury* would pay up to $1,000 for a story, but Faulkner just as often let *Story* magazine publish his work, so badly did he need the $25 that it paid. During these years, Faulkner's private life took some increasingly sad turns – one of which, it must be admitted, was his marriage to Estelle Oldham Franklin. Her divorce from Cornell in April 1929 brought her and their two children back to Oxford; she and Faulkner were married in June of that year, and Faulkner took full financial responsibility for the children. Neither the new husband nor the wife had the starry eyes of a first love any longer. Bill had had an unsuccessful relationship with Helen Baird in 1926; Estelle's marriage had failed. Both had begun to consume more alcohol than was good for them individually or as a couple. Bill devoted the most part of his interior life and a large portion of his time to his writing. Estelle, still a sociable woman, got lonely. In 1931 a daughter, Alabama, was born to them; she lived nine days, and Faulkner rode to the cemetery with her coffin on his knees. Two years later, their daughter Jill was born; she grew up in a home into which her father would not let her bring a record player. Their finances were strained by modernizing an antebellum home they bought in 1930, naming it Rowan Oak. In 1935 Faulkner's youngest brother, Dean, was killed while flying an airplane that Bill had bought him. The family, especially Maud and Bill, were devastated, and Dean's widow and namesake daughter soon moved into Rowan Oak. Faulkner captured the desperation of these years in a letter he wrote to one of his literary agents in 1940:

> Every so often, in spite of judgment and all else, I take these fits of sort of raging and impotent exasperation at this really quite alarming paradox which my life reveals: Beginning at the age of thirty I, an artist, a sincere one and of the first class, who should be free even of his own economic responsibilities and with no moral conscience at all, began to become the sole, principal and partial support – food, shelter, heat, clothes, medicine, kotex, school fees, toilet paper and picture shows – of my mother . . . [a] brother's widow and child, a wife of my own and two step children, my own child; I inherited my father's debts and his dependents, white and black without inheriting yet from anyone one inch of land or one stick of furniture or one cent of money; the only thing I ever got for nothing, after the first pair of long pants I received (cost: $7.50) was the

$300 O. Henry prize last year. I bought without help from anyone the
house I live in and all the furniture; I bought my farm the same way.
I am 42 years old and I have already paid for four funerals and will
certainly pay for one more and in all likelihood two more beside that,
provided none of the people in mine or my wife's family my superior
in age outlive me, before I ever come to my own.   (*SL* 122–3)

In 1935 Faulkner also began working as a scriptwriter at Twentieth Century-
Fox Studios, work which he did intermittently for the rest of the decade. At
the studios he met fellow southerner Meta Carpenter, and their intimate love
affair would continue on-and-off for fifteen years, interrupted by Meta's marriage to another man and complicated by Faulkner's marriage to Estelle and
commitment to Jill.

But if the 1930s and 1940s were difficult financially and emotionally, some
important recognition did begin to come Faulkner's way. He was elected to the
National Institute of Arts and Letters in 1939, and in 1944 he received a letter
from the literary critic Malcolm Cowley describing the project that would
infuse new life into his career. By that date Faulkner's novels had all gone
out of print; he remained virtually unread outside the literary community,
and he had a reputation as a difficult prose stylist. Max Perkins, who edited
Ernest Hemingway and F. Scott Fitzgerald for Scribner's publishing house,
said simply, "Faulkner is finished" (*FCF* 10). Cowley sought to change that
by getting the prestigious Viking Press to issue a volume on Faulkner in its
popular *Portable* series, which profiled writers by including a variety of pieces
by them. In Faulkner's case Cowley proposed that "Instead of trying to collect
the 'best of Faulkner' in 600 pages, I thought of selecting the short and long
stories, and passages from novels that are really separate stories, that form
part of your Mississippi series" (*FCF* 22). Delighted with the project, Faulkner
cooperated fully with its development, and the work hit only one serious snag:
Cowley's insistence on describing Faulkner's combat experience in the Great
War. Some of Faulkner's early posturing had reached print, and some of it was
just anecdotal, but Cowley believed that he had a war hero on his hands. "You're
going to bugger up a fine dignified book with that war business," Faulkner wrote
him; "If . . . you cant omit all European war reference, say only what Who's
Who says and no more: Was a member of the RAF in 1918." He even offered
to pay for any technical changes that had to be made in the process (*FCF* 82).

The Portable Faulkner (1946) did what Cowley had hoped. It was prominently
reviewed by novelists Caroline Gordon in the *New York Times Book Review* and
Robert Penn Warren in a two-part essay in the *New Republic*. These literary
admirers attracted new readers, and they coupled with an already appreciative
European reading public to increase Faulkner's status as an internationally

prominent writer. 1948 saw publication of Faulkner's novel *Intruder in the Dust* and the film version was shot in Oxford, Mississippi, where it had its international premiere in 1949. Faulkner had good use for the proceeds from both the film and the book, and at last the financial pressures on him began to abate.

When a Swedish reporter telephoned Rowan Oak in November 1950 to tell Faulkner that he had won the 1949 Nobel Prize for Literature, his years of obscurity were over for good. He initially declined to go to Stockholm to receive it, and he tried his best to duck the reporters intent on talking about it. His extended family ultimately conspired to get him to the ceremony, a process that a week-long hunting trip and a deliberate alcoholic binge threatened to derail. He decided to attend so that Jill could accompany him to Paris afterward, and during the attendant parties and dinners and the ceremony itself he was a model of good behavior. "I want to do the right thing," he said of the occasion (Blotner 532). Undoubtedly, the best "right thing" of the trip was the address he delivered upon receiving the Prize. No one present heard it, however, because he delivered it too far from the microphone and in a characteristically quiet and rushed manner, in a southern accent to boot. The next morning, when the text of the speech hit the news services, it was hailed as a masterpiece of rhetoric. It began by removing the occasion of the Prize from Faulkner's biography: "I feel that this award was not made to me as a man, but to my work – a life's work in the agony and sweat of the human spirit, not for glory and least of all for profit, but to create out of the materials of the human spirit something which did not exist before." Thus did he keep us out of his private life even as he explained something of what it meant to do the work – the very hard work – that he did. He invoked future winners of the Prize and spoke to them, to encourage them: "I believe that man will not only endure: he will prevail. He is immortal, not because he alone among creatures has an inexhaustible voice, but because he has a soul, a spirit capable of compassion and sacrifice and endurance. The poet's, the writer's, duty is to write about these things." He concluded with a gesture encompassing past and future: "The poet's voice need not merely be the record of man, it can be one of the props, the pillars to help him endure and prevail" (*ESPL* 119–20).

Faulkner scholars still debate the degree to which he meant those words and the relationship they bear to his fiction, particularly that which appeared after 1950. In the literary world winning the Nobel Prize is regarded as rather a jinx at best, and at worst a career-ending curse. Faulkner's literary production did slow down in the 1950s, but this was due in part to the difficulties he had in writing his most densely plotted and intricately written novel (*A Fable* [1954]) and in part to the increasing number of public duties he accepted as a Nobel laureate.

He also took public stands on the most important political movement in the America of his day – the civil rights movement and the dismantling of racial segregation in the American South. Thus the self-described "country man," "uneducated in every formal sense" (*SL* 348), deliberately took on the role of America's Spokesartist in the 1950s and at the same time inserted himself into incendiary political territory at home. The results were mixed. The US Department of State asked him to serve as a kind of literary ambassador to places such as Japan and Brazil; not least because of his reserved demeanor and polished public manners, he made a good one. His comments on the racial problems of America and the South pleased no one: to liberal whites, he did not protest loudly enough, and they condemned him as an accommodationist; to southern segregationists, he sounded crazy and dangerous, and they threatened his life and property; to some black southerners, he sounded just as crazy, and they stayed out of everyone's way; to other African Americans, he seemed like just another racist white man, and W. E. B. Du Bois even offered to debate with him on the steps of the courthouse in which Emmett Till's murderers had been acquitted by an all-white jury. Complicated in their conception and expression, Faulkner's ideas sprang from his belief in equal opportunity and in exercising personal responsibility in the pursuit of the same. He also deeply distrusted group behavior, and, as a symptom of that distrust, he had deep reservations about the federal government's power to effect change. At the University of Virginia, where he was Writer-in-Residence from 1957 to 1959, he told a delegation from the Department of Psychiatry:

> if I ever become a preacher, it will be to preach against man, individual man, relinquishing into groups, any groups . . . I think that there's too much pressure to make people conform and I think that one man may be first-rate but if you get one man and two second-rate men together, then he's not going to be first-rate any longer, because the voice of that majority will be a second-rate voice. (*FIU* 269)

At least snobbish and at most antidemocratic, such attitudes sprang from his own painful experiences of violated privacy. He did learn, finally, as his best biographer says, how to combine "avoidance and public relations." Asked in 1957 in Athens whether he had "a message for the Greek people," he said, "What message can anyone give to a people who is already the bravest and toughest and most independent people? Your country is the cradle of civilized man. Your ancestors are the mothers and fathers of civilization, and of human liberty. What more do you want of me, an American farmer?" (Blotner 636).

During the last five years or so of his life, Faulkner's deep and abiding thirst for alcohol began to have serious consequences for his health. The earliest descriptions we have of him note his desire to drink and his capacity to hold his liquor; accounts from his middle years record a pattern of binge drinking, sometimes deliberate, and always with certain patterns of entry, dissolution, and recovery. He sustained some serious injuries from these episodes. During one in New York in 1937, he fell against a pipe supplying steam heat to his hotel room, and by the time he was able to remove himself from it he had a third-degree burn on his back; the pain from that stayed with him for the rest of his life and was aggravated in his later years by falls from the horses he dearly loved to ride – and, against advice, to jump. A snide *New Yorker* profile of him at work in his editor's office in 1953 unwittingly captures both the physical effort that writing took and the pain he continued to inflict upon himself:

> we retreated to a corner to watch the sole owner and proprietor of Yoknapatawpha County bring forth prose. He typed very, *very* slowly, mostly with the middle finger of his right hand, but with an occasional assist from the index finger of his left . . . He lifted the sheet of paper in the typewriter and read over what he had written, then got up and stretched. "Work hurts mah back," he said.

The reporter did not know it, but he was recording the latter stages of Faulkner's epic struggle to finish *A Fable*; he did know that Faulkner attributed his pain to a fall from a horse and claimed that whiskey would cure what ailed him (*LIG* 75). After he finished writing what would be his last novel, *The Reivers* (1962), Faulkner said that he was "not working on anything at all now, busy with horses, fox hunting"; "I will wait until the stuff is ready, until I can follow instead of trying to drive it" (Blotner 697). By the time the Fourth of July dawned, however, he was drinking and taking prescription painkillers in response to the intense pain in his back. Before he began doing so, he had complained that food did not taste right. He agreed readily – for the first time ever to be taken to the sanitarium in nearby Byhalia to dry out. In that sanitarium, William Faulkner died of a heart attack.

The family issued a brief message before the funeral: "Until he's buried he belongs to the family. After that he belongs to the world" (Blotner 716). And – nineteen novels, more than a hundred short stories, many dozen poems and essays, and some line drawings and illustrated fables later, having traveled the world in reality and throughout the range of human experience in his imagination – so he does.

Chapter 2

Works

Everyone who reads or ever has read Faulkner has been confused by something. The long sentences, the elaborate syntax, the terrifying action, the obscure pronoun references: saying that his technique and style are difficult and his themes daunting seems like merely stating the obvious. The only way out of such confusion is to go through it. No shortcuts, no substitutes exist for the act of reading Faulkner; but reading Faulkner will teach you how to read Faulkner well. What follows in these pages therefore merely tries to sketch the parameters of his work and to point to areas of reflection on and discussion of this most challenging yet rewarding of modern writers.

Most of Faulkner's body of work is set primarily in the mythological county of Yoknapatawpha, Mississippi. Of the nineteen novels, only five are set elsewhere, and even these sometimes touch its borders: *Soldiers' Pay, Mosquitoes, Pylon, If I Forget Thee, Jerusalem (The Wild Palms)*, and *A Fable*. The chronology of his major published work reads as follows:

1919   First published poem, "L'Apres-Midi d'un Faune," in *The New Republic*; first published short story, "Landing in Luck," in *The Mississippian*

1924   *The Marble Faun* (poetry)

1926   *Soldiers' Pay* (novel)

1927   *Mosquitoes* (novel)

1929   *Sartoris* (novel); *The Sound and the Fury* (novel)

1930   *As I Lay Dying* (novel)

1931   *Sanctuary* (novel); *These 13* (short stories)

1932   *Light in August* (novel)

1933   *A Green Bough* (poetry)

1934   *Doctor Martino and Other Stories* (short stories)

1935   *Pylon* (novel)

1936   *Absalom, Absalom!* (novel)

1938   *The Unvanquished* (novel)

1939   *If I Forget Thee, Jerusalem (The Wild Palms)* (novel)

1940   *The Hamlet* (novel)

1942   *Go Down, Moses* (novel)

1946   *The Portable Faulkner* (compendium)

1948   *Intruder in the Dust* (novel)

1949   *Knight's Gambit* (short stories and a novella)

1950   *Collected Stories* (short stories)

1951   *Requiem for a Nun* (novel)

1954   *A Fable* (novel); *The Faulkner Reader* (compendium)

1955   *Big Woods* (short stories)

1957   *The Town* (novel)

1959   *The Mansion* (novel)

1962   *The Reivers* (novel)

Faulkner's uncollected stories, early poetry and prose, and nonfiction appeared posthumously. This chapter discusses each of his novels chronologically and his major short fiction and nonfiction afterward, in separate subsections.

Soldiers' Pay (1926)

This novel belongs to a period in American literature that reflected the dis-
illusionment of the generation who fought in and returned from the First
World War (1914–18), known then as the Great War. Ernest Hemingway used
Gertrude Stein's comment that this generation was "lost" as an epigraph to
his first novel, *The Sun Also Rises* (1926), and the tagline to describe an era
was born. The themes and techniques of early modernism, however, did not
originate with Faulkner and Hemingway but with the poets who came before
them, primarily Ezra Pound and T. S. Eliot, and with the Irish novelist and
prose innovator James Joyce. These writers experimented with ways to make
literary wholes out of fragments – of images, of sentences, of texts – and in
the process questioned whether any kind of wholeness was even possible in the
postwar era. That war had been conducted at great cost. The Allied Powers,
consisting primarily of Britain, France, Belgium, and (after 1917) the United
States lost eight million people, military and civilian; the Central Powers of
Germany and Austria-Hungary lost seven million. The Great War in Europe
was fought primarily in trenches, with the armed forces dug into the ground
and firing at one another from positions that could not be changed without
literally overrunning the opponent. In this war air combat came into its own,
and twenty-first-century tactics such as chemical warfare made their debut
alongside continued use of nineteenth-century forms such as the use of the
cavalry. The war completely changed the sensibilities of the Western world. As
Ezra Pound put it:

> These fought in any case,
> and some believing,
> . . .
> walked eye-deep in hell
> believing in old men's lies, then unbelieving
> came home, home to a lie,
> home to old lies and new infamy;
> . . .
> There died a myriad,
> And of the best, among them,
> For an old bitch gone in the teeth,
> For a botched civilization,
> . . .
> For two gross of broken statues,
> For a few thousand battered books.[1]

The male characters of *Soldiers' Pay* went to war "believing in old men's lies" and have come home to the American South with deep psychological and physical wounds that in turn damage the women they meet.

At the center of the novel's action sits Donald Mahon, an aviator shot down near the end of the war and horribly disfigured, whose condition provokes various reactions from those who meet him. Envied by a young cadet who had not seen combat, pitied by a young widow, protected by a toughened Army private, worshipped by his first love, and disdained by his shallow fiancée, Donald comes home to Georgia. His inevitable decline takes the measure of the other characters. Emmy, his first love, can only agonize at her distance from him; Mrs Powers agrees to marry him because she feels guilty for falling out of love with her own husband before he died. His father, an elderly rector, clings to the belief that his only child will recover. Joe Gilligan becomes a valet-turned-nurse for the ruined pilot in part so that he can stay near Mrs Powers. Among them travel a host of silly, salacious, and sanctimonious minor players whose choices nonetheless revolve around Donald's status. These characters also provide occasion for Faulkner to exercise his sense of humor and his literary knowledge. The "goatlike" Januarius Jones, for example, whose lechery is exceeded only by his self-esteem, does battle for a flapper's attention while telling egregious lies about his background: "like Henry James, he attained verisimilitude by means of tediousness."[2] We first meet him "baggy in gray tweed," "watching April busy in a hyacinth bed" (56) – a nod to Eliot's beginning of *The Waste Land* (1922). *Soldiers' Pay* is very much a self-consciously literary first novel by a writer as intent on demonstrating what he knew about and thought of other writers as he was on producing a novel of the modern age.

Yet *Soldiers' Pay* also contains passages of beautiful, highly poetic prose and strikingly revelatory moments of character development that make it more than just a book to read because the man who wrote it eventually created Yoknapatawpha County. For example, Faulkner narrates the moment of Donald Mahon's death from Donald's point of view and casts it as a reliving of the moment he was wounded in France: "His father's heavy face hung over him in the dusk like a murdered Caesar's. He knew sight again and an imminent nothingness more profound than any yet, while evening, like a ship with twilight-colored sails, drew down the world, putting calmly out to an immeasurable sea. 'That's how it happened,' he said, staring at him" (294). After a rather clumsy apostrophe to "sex and death: the front door and the back door of the world," Faulkner returns his trust to his characters and their responses to life and closes the novel focused on "All the longing of mankind for a Oneness with Something, somewhere" as Reverend Mahon and Joe Gilligan listen to the singing in a black church: "They stood together in the dust, the rector in his shapeless black, and Gilligan in his new hard serge, listening, seeing the shabby church become beautiful with mellow longing, passionate and sad . . . and they turned townward under the moon, feeling dust in their shoes" (319).

Mosquitoes (1927)

In his second novel Faulkner turned deeper south, to New Orleans, the city in which he had become friends with Sherwood Anderson. That writer had helped to usher American fiction into the modern age with *Winesburg, Ohio* (1919), a collection of short stories that examined the psychological damage and spiritual vacuity of the inhabitants of a town in middle America. Faulkner greatly admired Anderson and always credited him with inspiring him to write and helping him to publish his first novel. *Mosquitoes* takes as its subject the artistic world of postwar New Orleans – the very world that Faulkner and Anderson briefly inhabited – in which the erstwhile patroness Mrs Maurier assembles a diverse yacht party of artists and other ne'er-do-wells. Faulkner then runs the yacht into a sandbar, stranding it there until help can arrive, during which time the most loquacious of the characters discuss Art and What It Means, while the others discover and pursue sexual fantasies, including lesbian and homoerotic ones. Indeed, the novel begins by conflating the two efforts of sex and talk. Mr Talliaferro, an obsequious fraud, sits trying to impress a sculptor in conversation: "'The sex instinct,' repeated Mr Talliaferro in his careful cockney, with that smug complacence with which you plead guilty to a characteristic which you privately consider a virtue, 'is quite strong in me.'"[3] The novel nods often at other modern artists who have considered these questions. Mrs Maurier's yacht is called the *Nausikaa*, an allusion to an episode of James Joyce's *Ulysses* (1922), and the novel begins as "Spring and the cruellest months were gone" (2), an echo of the most famous lines of Eliot's *The Waste Land* (1922). Both a serious meditation on art and a satire of those who substitute it for involvement with the real, physical world, the novel has no single source of authority on these matters, no one character who speaks for Faulkner. Rather, Faulkner's point is that human life is not so neatly divided between the physical and the intellectual as his characters would have it. Faulkner scholars have tended to see *Mosquitoes* as thinly veiled autobiography (as they did *Soldiers' Pay*) and as failed fiction of his "apprenticeship" in literature. Recent criticism, however, has suggested that Faulkner blurred the lines between the erotic and the aesthetic in order to explore the roles that culture plays in shaping matters as personal as sexual identity. Indeed, he seems to have been ahead of his time in representing various demands placed upon males to be "men" and females to be "women," whatever those things mean in a given social order at a given time. The discovery and publication of four deleted scenes further indicates that his great theme about human mutability seems to have been undermined by editors worried about controversial scenes describing sex and talking about it. Those scenes have been restored to the most recent edition of the novel.[4]

Sartoris/Flags in the Dust (1929)

Sartoris was not finally shaped by Faulkner but by his friend Ben Wasson, who edited it when the longer manuscript *Flags in the Dust* had been rejected twice by publishers as too diffuse and disorganized. *Sartoris* thus became Faulkner's third published novel. In 1973 his publishers released an edition of *Flags*, and the novel has recently been reedited under that title. Owing to some gaps in the typesetting record, we still do not have a version of the novel that Faulkner finally made, although he did accept *Sartoris* as Wasson crafted it and made no attempts during his lifetime to publish *Flags* in its entirety. Students wishing to read the first novel set in what would come to be called Yoknapatawpha County have a dilemma: which text to choose?

Readers of either version will find members of the Sartoris and Benbow families, and will discover the complicated ways in which they meet and mesh. The novels both begin with the current patriarch of the Sartoris family, Bayard, in conversation with a longtime crony. However, *Sartoris* directly invokes the "spirit"[5] of Bayard's father John, the "real" head of the family, while *Flags* more subtly brings John into the room while Old Man Falls tells an anecdote about him from the Civil War. From the beginning, then, *Flags* works indirectly toward its themes and *Sartoris* states them more explicitly. As the title suggests, *Sartoris* concerns the history of one family and its decline over time. The main action of the plot traces Bayard's grandson's return from the Great War and the self-destructive behavior in which he indulges because of the guilt he feels at his twin brother's death during the war. The entire family and its black servants are thrown into disarray by the younger Bayard's return. He marries Narcissa Benbow and fathers a son; he also kills his grandfather in an automobile accident and, finally, himself in an unstable airplane. Both novels end after Miss Jenny, the older Bayard's aunt, visits the dead Sartoris men in the graveyard and returns home only to learn that her great-great-great nephew has not been named, like the generations before him, either Bayard or John: "His name is Benbow Sartoris," Narcissa says (302).[6] Miss Jenny believes that

Narcissa is trying to "change one of 'em with a name." In *Flags* the effect of Narcissa's news is sad because of the subtle appearance of the title in the closing paragraphs: "perhaps Sartoris is the name of the game itself . . . for there is death in the sound of it, and a glamorous fatality, like silver pennons downrushing at sunset, or a dying fall of horns along the road to Roncevaux" (432–3). In *Sartoris* Narcissa's action seems more deliberately malicious: "Narcissa played on as though she were not listening. Then she turned her head and without ceasing her hands, she smiled at Miss Jenny quietly, a little dreamily, with serene fond detachment" (433). It is as though she intends to end the powerful lure of two men – her husband and his twin before him – whom she could not resist.

The Benbow family also figures prominently in *Sanctuary* (1931), which Faulkner was writing as he finished *Flags in the Dust* and worked on what would become *The Sound and the Fury*, published like *Sartoris* in 1929. Moreover, *Flags* shares with *Mosquitoes* a focus on taboo forms of sexuality. After two rejections, Faulkner gave Wasson the manuscript to place with a publisher, and the twelfth one agreed to print it if cuts were made to it. Wasson made those cuts, shortening the manuscript by about a quarter. When he did so, he cut a great deal of the scenes that investigate taboos, including those of lawyer Horace Benbow's sexual interest in his own sister and an affair that Horace has with the sister of the woman he marries, herself married to someone else when her affair with Horace begins. Depressed about the slow publication process, engrossed with two new projects, and always impatient of making alterations that might please editors, Faulkner agreed to Wasson's changes, but he would never again give over a whole novel to an editor for first aid. In fact, when Wasson sent Faulkner the proofs of *The Sound and the Fury*, complete with his own edits, Faulkner sent them back corrected to his original, writing in a cover letter, "And dont[7] make any more additions to the script, bud. I know you mean well, but so do I" (*SL* 45). Because most readers prefer to read the version that Faulkner wanted us to read, then, most readers prefer *Flags in the Dust*, indirections, conflicting editions, taboos, and all.

The Sound and the Fury (1929)

Yes, there are two Quentins in this novel; and yes, one of them is a girl.

First-time readers of Faulkner's fourth, and arguably his most famous, novel always ask the two questions behind those two answers because the novel begins with the first-person narration of a character who knows two Quentins but cannot distinguish between the time periods in which he knows them. To Benjy, the first of the three Compson brothers who will speak from these pages, life exists in an eternal present tense. He responds to every event in his life as though it were happening for the first time. Because he cannot distinguish past from present or look forward to a future, he cannot think causally, and because he cannot move from an action to its consequence, he cannot interpret for us, and we are lost. We can find meaning in Benjy's section only by rereading it after we have read the novel's last page, for *The Sound and the Fury* contains many mysteries. The first of these emerges from the source of the novel's title:

> Tomorrow, and tomorrow, and tomorrow
> Creeps in this petty pace from day to day,
> To the last syllable of recorded time,
> And all our yesterdays have lighted fools
> The way to dusty death. Out, out, brief candle!
> Life's but a walking shadow, a poor player
> That struts and frets his hour upon the stage
> And then is heard no more. It is a tale
> Told by an idiot, full of sound and fury
> Signifying nothing.   (*Macbeth* V.v.19–28)

Shakespeare's Macbeth speaks these lines on learning that his wife and co-conspirator in the murder of a king has committed suicide. He is beyond despair, beyond hope, beyond life itself: he is finished. Faulkner's title thus raises questions for the novel at the outset. This tale begins with a "tale told by an idiot" and moves successively through the narratives of his two brothers, one a suicide and one a selfish misanthrope, to conclude in the words of an omniscient narrator describing Benjy's wailing voice as "horror; shock; agony eyeless, tongueless; just sound."[8] Macbeth would say that all of this signifies nothing, makes no difference in the inevitable march toward death.

Does Faulkner's novel reach a similar conclusion? A brief review of the plot might suggest that it does. The four children of Caroline and Jason Compson grow up in their family's antebellum house during the last years of the nineteenth century and the first of the twentieth. They list a governor of Mississippi and a Civil War general among their ancestors; their mother is a class-conscious snob and their father an alcoholic. The only girl among them gets pregnant out of wedlock; the oldest child kills himself at the end of his freshman year at Harvard; the youngest never grows mentally or emotionally past the age of three; the one who stays at home torments everyone within reach, including his illegitimate niece, who finally robs him and runs off with a carnival worker. These very bare bones of the plot emerge from four present-tense days in the novel arranged as follows: April 7, 1928; June 2, 1910; April 6, 1928; and April 8, 1928, which also serve as chapter titles. This overall structure asks us to ask why Faulkner disjointed chronology like this, why he did not just tell us what happened. Its structure, like its title, asks us to participate in solving a mystery.

In such participation lies the key to all of Faulkner's fiction, not just *The Sound and the Fury*. Such participation is the act of interpretation itself, and Faulkner would have us do that rather than do it for us; in this way he makes the act of reading as creative as the act of writing and as important to the life represented in the aesthetic object. The dichotomy in *Mosquitoes* between art and life he thus transforms in *The Sound and the Fury* into paradox, and paradox would ever after be the defining quality of his imagination and his art. In an interview he gave in 1955, he averred that "The aim of every artist is to arrest motion, which is life, by artificial means and hold it fixed so that 100 years later when a stranger looks at it, it moves again since it is life" (*LIG* 253). He made it sound so simple, but it was in writing the very complex pages of *The Sound and the Fury* nearly thirty years before that he made the discovery.

To begin thinking fruitfully about how this process works in this novel, we can ask questions of the first-person narrators. By finding their strengths and limitations, we can move to an analysis of how matters look from the omniscient point of view in the final section and ask what we gain and lose with that perspective. Finally, we can see what emerges as common between the sections, and we can read between them to see what, if anything, they mean.

Benjy seems at first like an unreliable narrator because he cannot interpret what he sees. In fact, that characteristic makes him an extremely reliable narrator because he can neither lie to us nor deceive himself. He might not think rationally, but he does know things, initially by their physical attributes. In the creek with Luster in 1928, for example, Benjy remembers "playing in the branch and Caddy squatted down and got her dress wet" (17) and a character named Versh scolding her for it. When he remembers Versh taking him around the corner of the kitchen, he remembers someone named T. P. doing the same thing. Even a first reading creates the impression that Luster, Versh, and T. P. are Benjy's black caretakers but that Benjy is happiest when he is with his sister Caddy, "who smelled like trees." At one point Luster, frustrated with Benjy's constant noise, says "Beller. You want something to beller about. All right, then. Caddy" (55). Consequently we can infer that when Benjy is with Luster, Caddy is long gone, and Benjy wants her. Other physical acts or conditions, like weather or getting his clothing caught on a nail in the fence, cause Benjy's mind to jump to a scene with the same physical trigger. To Benjy, an absence of something he wants is just such a trigger. He hears a golfer cry, "Here, caddie" and cries for his Caddy (3). He undresses for bed and "I looked at myself, and I began to cry," and Luster tells us why: "Looking for them aint going to do no good. They're gone" (73). He gets into bed with Luster and remembers getting into bed with Caddy, who "held me and I could hear us all, and the darkness, and something I could smell" and "the dark began to go in smooth, bright shapes, like it always does, even when Caddy says that I have been asleep" (75).

Because Benjy cannot distinguish past from present, we must, and Faulkner gives us the means by which to do so. Benjy records other people's voices exactly, for example. He may not understand what they say, but in his repetitions of their words he copies their speech patterns and mannerisms, which we learn to recognize precisely because of the repetitions that he cannot help but make:

> "I told you Mother was crying," Quentin said. Versh took me up and
> opened the door onto the back porch. We went out and Versh closed
> the door black. I could smell Versh and feel him. You all be quiet, now.
> We're not going up stairs yet. Mr Jason said for you to come right up
> stairs. He said to mind me. I'm not going to mind you. But he said for
> all of us to. Didn't he, Quentin. I could feel Versh's head. I could hear
> us. Didn't he, Versh. Yes, that right. Then I say for us to go out doors
> a while. Come on. Versh opened the door and we went out.   (27)

Because we get no help from Benjy, we start to pay attention to those around him and to how they respond to him and to each other. Therefore, in passages like the one above, we note that Versh calls their father "Mr" and the children ignore his reminder of Mr Compson's directions; we see oldest child Quentin's mental distance from the others and ask "Why?" of both observations. In the former we infer that Versh's status as a black servant allows the children to ignore even their father's orders. By the end of Benjy's section, when he describes Quentin crying and turning his back to the room as he gets into bed (73–4), we realize that Quentin knows more about the adult situation than the other children do. He knows that the singing in the parlor is not because his grandmother is sick, as they have been told, but because she has died.

Reading beyond the lines of the limited text provided by the narrator creates meaning that the narrator cannot – or, in the cases of Quentin and Jason, will not – give us. Quentin, too, is obsessed with absences. Taking to heart his father's contention that sexual virginity is "like death: only a state in which the others are left," Quentin quickly conflates his sister Caddy's absence from his life with the absence of sex from his life: "Why couldn't it have been me and not her who is unvirgin" (78). If Benjy likes his sister to smell like trees and grieves when she wears perfume and kisses boys, then Quentin obsesses over the moment at which she passes forever into adulthood and sexuality, leaving her older brother behind. At one point he even wishes that he could have been Caddy's lover's mother, "lying with open body lifted laughing, holding his father with my hand refraining, seeing, watching him die before he lived" (81) – in effect, denying his sister her sexuality by becoming the woman who declined impregnation. Such tortuous (and tortured) reflection marks Quentin's section, and his tendency to narrate what he did not do as well as what he has done makes his narration unstable on nearly every front. Quentin knows when he wakes up on June 2, 1910, that he will drown himself that evening, and he spends the entire day contemplating that ultimate of absences – himself from the world. As the longest of the novel's four sections builds toward its conclusion, then, Quentin draws closer toward the memory that will literally push him over the edge of life into the state that his father has equated with sexual experience.

The fact that Quentin kills himself takes all first-time readers by surprise because his section ends with his matter-of-fact description of getting ready to go out for the evening. Immediately before that ending, however, stands his memory of a conversation with his father in which he confessed to committing incest with Caddy – a conversation that occurred about an event that did not. He has checked the time compulsively all day, in shadows as well as clocks, and in the evening bells he hears "A quarter hour yet. And then I'll not be. The peacefullest words. Peacefullest words" (174). With the final minutes of his life in place, Quentin slips into the memory of his most important conversation with the man who taught his children that "all men are just accumulations dolls stuffed with sawdust swept up from the trash heaps where all previous dolls had been thrown away" (175). Against such undeviating nihilism, Quentin tries to assert the hope that "people could change one another forever" and that sex could let them "merge like a flame swirling up for an instant then blown cleanly out along the cool eternal dark" instead of consisting of its more quotidian aspects (176). If he could make his father believe that they had committed incest, Quentin thinks, he could at last stand counted as important: so powerful is Mr Compson in his son's psyche that "if I could tell you we did it would have been so" (177). When his father dismisses the confession and Quentin's wrenched emotional state, with its overt threat of suicide, as a "temporary state of mind," Quentin fixes on that word among all the others in the elder's soliloquy of man's worthlessness. He replays the conversation with his own incredulous refrain: "and i temporary," he repeats, in a phrase that underscores his very self as just that.

Quentin longs to exert a powerful, permanent effect on some aspect of life, and he focuses his attentions on his sister because she seems to him to have done this. Ironically, Caddy has only done the natural thing: she has grown up. Her father's dismissal of her sexuality and her mother's frantic attempts to marry her off before her potential husband can learn to count equally restrict her position in the Compson house, and her options in life; her three brothers' attempts to prolong one of the stages of her life to suit their own ends makes life anywhere for her virtually untenable. That tragic reality appears most fully in her brother Jason's section of *The Sound and the Fury*. It opens with "Once a bitch, always a bitch, what I say," and although in that context he refers to the niece named after his dead brother, he means every woman he knows, with the possible exception of his girlfriend, a whore named Lorraine. Jason's section is everywhere characterized by absences and obsessions, just like the sections narrated by his brothers, but because of his savage (and extremely funny) voice and demeanor, Jason attracts less readerly sympathy than Benjy and Quentin. That very fact acts as a caution to look beneath Jason's cruelty for its sources and to ask again what he tells us that the others cannot or will not.

Jason's misogyny and racism obviously disqualify him as an admirable person, but he is not uncomplicated psychologically. In fact, he goes to great lengths to hide his most important longings from himself, and therefore from us, a kind of psychic depth that Benjy and Quentin do not share. His clearest obsessions are with his niece's body and the job he lost in the bank when Caddy's marriage to Herbert Head fell apart, but he is equally obsessed with his parents, who enter his mind unbidden and in the unlikeliest of contexts. While he pursues his niece on the day of his narration, Quentin and his mother and his employer all merge into one antagonist:

> I dont owe anything to anybody that has no more consideration for me, that wouldn't be a dam bit above planting that ford there and making me spend a whole afternoon and Earl taking her back there and showing her the books just because he's too dam virtuous for this world. I says you'll have one hell of a time in heaven, without anybody's business to meddle in only dont you ever let me catch you at it I says, I close my eyes to it because of your grandmother, but just you let me catch you doing it one time on this place, where my mother lives. (241)

Jason's anger and self-righteousness shield him from admitting how much of his self-esteem derives from his place at the head of the Compson household, a place he took from his father Jason, whose death he still cannot remember without grief and anger. In the following passages he cannot bring himself even to say the word "funeral," for example: warning his mother that Caddy will try to see her daughter, he says, "If you believe she'll do what she says and not try to see it, you fool yourself because the first time that was the Mother kept on saying thank God you are not a Compson except in name" (196); of his uncle's drinking he says, "I reckon the least he could do at Father's or maybe the sideboard thought it was still Father and tripped him up when he passed" (197). Allowing himself to remember that day, Jason recalls the covered grave and says, "I began to feel sort of funny," and with Caddy beside him, "I got to thinking about when we were little and one thing and another and I got to feeling funny again, kind of mad or something" (202, 203). He cannot acknowledge real grief or loss, so he rants against imagined wrongs done him. And he is the great actor on the stage of his own life. He has all the clever comebacks, the witty one-liners that finish off discussion and argument, with his great mantra "I says." But close inspection reveals that he does not really say many of the things he says he does:

> Then she says, "I'll be gone soon. I know I'm just a burden to you" and I says "You've been saying that so long that I'm beginning to believe you" only I says you'd better be sure and not let me know you're gone because I'll sure have him on number seventeen that night and I says I think I know a place they'll take her too and the name of it's not Milk street and Honey avenue either. Then she begun to cry and I says all right all right I have as much pride about my kinfolks as anybody even if I dont always know where they come from.   (222)
> "No," I says. "You wouldn't know. And you can thank your stars for that," I says. Only what would be the use in saying it aloud. It would just have her crying on me again.   (263)

His insistence on rhetorical power masks a fragile ego, and Faulkner lets one character puncture it – the elderly black man who also works in the hardware store. "You fools a man whut so smart he cant even keep up wid hisself," Old Job tells him, and when Jason asks "Who's that?" "'Dat's Mr Jason Compson,' he says" (250).

When Dilsey opens the door to her cabin at the beginning of the fourth section of *The Sound and the Fury*, readers at last get a chance to see the characters. Benjy, Quentin, and Jason have no need to describe people they know so well. The omniscient narrator, on the other hand, shows us Dilsey in her Sunday finery; Benjy with his fine, pale hair and eyes "the sweet pale blue of cornflowers" (274); and Jason and his mother across the table from one another in "identical attitudes," "the one cold and shrewd" and "the other cold and querulous" (279). The narrator cannot describe young Quentin because she has stolen Jason's secret cache of money and run away with a man who works for a traveling carnival. The smugness evident throughout April 6, his section, disappears when Jason makes this discovery. His attempt to catch Quentin fails miserably, and people on their way to Easter services on April 8 see "the man sitting quietly behind the wheel of a small car, with his invisible life ravelled out about him like a wornout sock" (313). Embedded in the story of the Compson family's end is the story of Dilsey Gibson and her thankless job as caretaker. She attends Easter services and brings Benjy along, and she believes the spirit of the Bible that Caroline Compson uses mainly as a prop in her sickbed. Her presence in the novel offers some readers reassurance that the world of this novel is not all bleakness and greed, that some hope exists. Dilsey clearly believes that the real world is the next, but none of her belief changes the Compson reality one bit; the salvation she finds in the Easter service stands in ironic contrast to the lives of people who use Sunday morning to sleep late. To make this point Faulkner closes the novel with a scene of crisis averted. When Luster drives Benjy the wrong way around the town square during his weekly trip to the graveyard, Benjy becomes completely disoriented and starts to bellow. Hearing his "voice mounting toward its unbelievable crescendo," Jason hauls the horse and wagon aright, and the novel closes as the shapes of the world assume their proper place in Benjy's perspective. The tale ends as it began, in the mind of an idiot.

Faulkner often said in interviews that *The Sound and the Fury* was "the book I feel tenderest towards" because he tried to tell it five times and failed each time (*LIG* 222, 244–5). The fifth time was a piece he wrote for Malcolm Cowley's *The Portable Faulkner* (1946). Known now as the Compson Appendix, the piece traces the Compson family from eighteenth-century Scotland to the mid-twentieth-century South. The Appendix prefaces some editions of the novel and acts as an Afterword to others, while in some it does not appear at all. Some readers choose to interpret the events of the novel according to the Appendix, but it seems more accurate to read the novel as a product of Faulkner's imagination in the late 1920s and the Appendix as a product of his imagination in the mid-1940s. Interestingly, he tried yet another persona through which to view his vexed family, "a sort of bloodless bibliophile's point of view," "a sort of Garter King-at-Arms, heatless, not very moved, cleaning up 'Compson' before going on to the next 'C-o' or 'C-r'" (*SL* 206). This narrator is not interested in the kind of participatory reading that takes place between and among the sections of *The Sound and the Fury;* this kind of narration assumes that facts are facts and writing is mere transcription. Even Benjy knows that communication consists of more than that, and in his memory of his castration we see the tremendous stakes in any effort to speak:

> I was trying to say, and I caught her, trying to say, and she screamed and I was trying to say and trying and the bright shapes began to stop and I tried to get out. I tried to get it off my face, but the bright shapes were going again. They were going up the hill to where it fell away and I tried to cry. But when I breathed in, I couldn't breathe out again to cry, and I tried to keep from falling off the hill and I fell off the hill into the bright, whirling shapes.   (53)

Every page of this novel contains people "trying to say," and that of course is what novelists do by profession. What if, like Benjy, you try to say, and fail? What if your language, any language, is just sound and fury that signifies nothing?

If Macbeth was right, why write at all?

As I Lay Dying (1930)

Faulkner names his mythical Mississippi county in this novel, his fifth. After the druggist Moseley refuses to help young Dewey Dell Bundren end her pregnancy, he describes secondhand the rest of her family, who have brought their mother's corpse through town on their way to Jefferson:

> It had been dead eight days, Albert said. They came from someplace out in Yoknapatawpha County, trying to get to Jefferson with it. It must have been like a piece of rotten cheese coming into an ant-hill, in that ramshackle wagon that Albert said folks were scared would fall all to pieces before they could get it out of town, with that home-made box and another fellow with a broken leg lying on a quilt on top of it, and the father and a little boy sitting on the seat and the marshal trying to make them get out of town.[9]

Fifteen narrators tell the story of the Bundrens' trip to Jefferson. The family members include Anse, the shiftless father; the oldest son Cash, a fine carpenter; the next-oldest, Darl; the middle child Jewel; the only daughter, Dewey Dell; the youngest child, Vardaman; and the dead Addie herself. They are joined in the narration by neighbors and strangers alike. Darl narrates the most chapters, with nineteen, followed by Vardaman with ten; some characters, like the above-quoted Moseley and the hot-tempered Jewel, narrate only one. Faulkner clearly wants not only to tell the story of Addie's strange funeral procession but also to raise questions about the processes and responsibilities of narration itself.

As I Lay Dying uses its multiple narrators to texture the world in which the Bundrens live and through which they move. As readers, we sift through the voices to find out whom to trust, which version of narrative to believe. Obviously, we will not believe someone who lies to us, as neighbor Cora Tull does when she claims that Darl asked his father and brother not to leave Addie's sickbed in order to sell a load of lumber: "He said Darl almost begged them on his knees not to force him to leave her in her condition, but nothing would do but Anse and Jewel must make that three dollars" (22). But three pages earlier, Darl himself has told us that he urged the trip: "It means three dollars . . . Do you want us to go, or not? . . . We'll be back by tomorrow sundown" (19).

Similarly, Anse's narration is suspect, his behavior as self-serving as Cora's. He blames all of his troubles on the road outside his door because when God "aims for something to be always a-moving, He makes it long ways, like a road or a horse or a wagon, but when He aims for something to stay put, He makes it up-and-down ways, like a tree or a man" (36). Trouble finds Anse on that road:

> me without a tooth in my head, hoping to get ahead enough so I could get my mouth fixed where I could eat God's own victuals as a man should . . . And now I can see same as second sight the rain shutting down betwixt us, a-coming up that road like a durn man, like it want ere a other house to rain on in all the living land.   (37–8)

As everyone in the novel knows, Anse's road is just an excuse for laziness, as Cash implies: "Sometimes I think that if a working man could see work as far ahead as a lazy man can see laziness" (236). Anse takes trouble on the road when Addie dies and he fulfills his promise to bury her with her kinfolks in Jefferson: "'God's will be done,' he says, 'Now I can get them teeth'" (52).

Yet sometimes we have no such points of comparison by which to judge a narrator's version of events. Darl, for example, seems like the sensitive member of the family; his philosophical and reflective nature appeals to likeminded readers. He dwells in border states of the imagination: "Beyond the unlamped wall I can hear the rain shaping the wagon that is ours, the load that is no longer theirs that felled and sawed it nor yet theirs that bought it and which is not ours either" (80); "How often have I lain beneath rain on a strange roof, thinking of home" (81). Yet Darl has a cruel streak. He can communicate telepathically with Jewel, Dewey Dell, and Cash, and he often torments the former two in that way. He taunts Jewel over Addie's impending death, and he "said he knew without the words" about Dewey Dell's pregnancy, and she hates him for it. By the end of the novel, his personality has split entirely in two, and one half can imagine the other "in a cage in Jackson where, his grimed hands lying light in the quiet interstices, looking out he foams" (254). To this unstable personality Faulkner entrusts the only description of Addie's death in the novel, thus complicating the emerging portraits of madness, sanity, artistry, and clairvoyance and collapsing the lines between them. As Cash says, "Sometimes I aint so sho who's got ere a right to say when a man is crazy and when he aint. Sometimes I think it aint none of us pure crazy and aint none of us pure sane until the balance of us talks him that-a-way" (233). In spite of that sympathy, Cash thinks Darl must go to the asylum because he has set fire to a barn in which the coffin was housed. If the ever-practical Cash is right, the world has no room for people like Darl – crazy or clairvoyant, he threatens the order of the material world, and he must go "Because there just aint nothing justifies the deliberate destruction of what a man has built with his own sweat and stored the fruit of his sweat into" (238).

Critics have long noted that each member of the Bundren family has his or her own reason to go to Jefferson, aside from burying Addie. Anse wants his teeth, Dewey Dell an abortion, Cash a graphophone, Vardaman some bananas. This list exempts Jewel and Darl and highlights them as exceptions to whatever rule operates in the Bundren family. We discover that Jewel, for instance, who looks so different from the other children, is in fact not Anse's son but the product of Addie's affair with Reverend Whitfield. Of all the children, only he seems to want to protect his mother from death: "It would be just me and her on a high hill and me rolling the rocks down the hill at their faces" (15). The other children have long known Jewel as their mother's favorite; he and Darl are often at odds, with Darl and Cash siding together as a sibling team, Dewey Dell aside and Vardaman too young to understand complicated family dynamics. Darl stands apart from the others precisely because of the characteristics that make him a good (if unreliable) narrator. He tends to dream and to record his various musings. Yet he depends on his family for security as surely as Anse relies on them for labor. He is as willing to fight for the family honor as the hot-headed Jewel (229–31), and his personality splits not because Anse and Dewey Dell want to send him to the asylum but because Cash did not tell him about that plan: "I thought you would have told me," Darl says, "I never thought you wouldn't have" (237). For all their individual limitations, the Bundrens function extremely well as a unit until one of them destroys someone's property.

That the material world trumps the imaginative one in this way suggests Faulkner's abiding interest in the fate of the artist in the world. Whether he is right to try to burn Addie's decaying body or not, Darl is crushed, and the lesson will not be lost on Vardaman, who spends so much of this novel trying to express his identity both as a son to a dead woman and as an individual. Trying to understand "an *is* different from my *is*," Vardaman equates the moment that he saw a fish die with the moment that he saw his mother die: "I saw when it did not be her" (56, 66). He comes to believe that the essence of his mother has escaped, and he knows where it went: "My mother is a fish," he reasons, in the novel's most famous chapter (84). Opposite the portrait of Vardaman's emerging identity, Faulkner sets one of identity finished and frozen. Addie Bundren has deliberately stopped developing as a person. Her chapter tells us that she was raised by the most nihilistic man since Jason Compson, Senior: "my father used to say that the reason for living was to get ready to stay dead a long time" (169). She became a schoolteacher who looked forward to beating her pupils, so starved for human connection was she, and she married Anse in response to her unfulfilled sexual desire: "In the early spring it was worst" (170). When she became pregnant Addie "learned that words were no good; that words dont ever fit even what they are trying to say at" (171), and that distrust of language parallels her deep distrust of other people not of her blood: "I gave Anse the children," she says, "I would be I; I would let him be the shape and echo of his word" (174). Ironically, the "word" she so discredits provides her with her "revenge" when she makes Anse promise to bury her in Jefferson: "my revenge would be that he would never know I was taking revenge" (173). However, Addie's feelings about language change when she falls in love with Reverend Whitfield, and when the affair ends, her old cynicism redoubles: "I gave Anse Dewey Dell to negative Jewel. Then I gave him Vardaman to replace the child I had robbed him of. And now he has three children that are his and not mine. And then I could get ready to die" (176). She is the novel's title character, the Clytemnestra described in the *Odyssey* by Agamemnon in the underworld: "As I lay dying the woman with the dog's eyes would not close my eyes for me as I descended into Hades" (Book XI). Given Addie's father's definition of "living" as "getting ready to stay dead for a long time," the book's title and Addie's chapter imply that dying and living are the same hopeless, pointless, doomed processes.

But the novel does not end with Addie's chapter, and it only begins with the title. The Bundren family heals itself after it sends Darl to Jackson: Anse finds a new Mrs Bundren; Dewey Dell and Vardaman get a new mother; Cash even gets to listen to new records on the woman's graphophone. Technically, then, *As I Lay Dying* is a comedy in the Shakespearean sense. It ends with disrupting forces purged and order restored – a marriage. And the book contains some of Faulkner's funniest writing and most unforgettable characters. When Doctor Peabody has to undo the Bundrens' first aid on Cash's broken leg, for instance, he huffs:

> "And dont tell me it aint going to bother you to lose sixty-odd square inches of skin to get that concrete off . . . God Almighty, why didn't Anse carry you to the nearest sawmill and stick your leg in the saw? That would have cured it. Then you all could have stuck his head into the saw and cured a whole family." (240)

Faulkner himself often described the novel as a "*tour de force*," meaning a show of strength or virtuosity that "just came all of a piece with no work on my part. Just came like that. I just thought of all the natural catastrophes that could happen to a family and let them all happen" (*LIG* 222). In such a show it seems fitting that he would name his county so offhandedly – in a passing reference, by a character who appears only once in his fiction, that waves away the differences between the created and the material worlds. "Beginning with *Sartoris*," he would say later, "I discovered that my own little postage stamp of native soil was worth writing about and that I would never live long enough to exhaust it, and by sublimating the actual to the apocryphal I would have complete liberty to use whatever talent I might have to its absolute top" (*LIG* 255). With *As I Lay Dying*, the apocryphal got an actual name, which Faulkner always translated as "water runs slow through flat land" and credited to the Chickasaws of Lafayette County and thereabouts, thus layering the two realms yet again.

Sanctuary (1931)

With its origins in the *Flags in the Dust* manuscript, *Sanctuary* was written between *The Sound and the Fury* and *As I Lay Dying*. The book's most recent editor notes that "*Sanctuary* is without question the work that has been most heavily revised by the author himself."[10] Faulkner told a story about its composition that, while not exactly true, reveals the status of that book as an ongoing work-in-progress; he said that his editor read the manuscript and said that if he printed it they would both go to jail, so he revised it to make it less sensationalistic. Scholarship has shown that Faulkner did pay to revise the book late in the publication process, but such revision merely continued his narrative experimentation rather than seeking to correct or clean up his material. (Indeed, he made the novel more graphic and sensational, not less.) That material concerns, among other things, the rape and abduction of a young college student, Temple Drake, the only daughter of a Jefferson judge; the illegal liquor and prostitution trade in north Mississippi and Memphis and the gangsters who run it; and the failing marriage of a local attorney and his attendant crush on his stepdaughter. Along the way two innocent men are murdered, a local politician prowls the underworld, and perjury leads to a lynching. Perhaps not surprisingly, "the most horrific tale I could imagine" (323) sold more copies than *The Sound and the Fury* and *As I Lay Dying* combined.

Throughout the novel, Faulkner uses a sliding, omniscient perspective, a flexible approach that can highlight individual perceptions without surrendering entirely to the limitations imposed by individual voices and personalities. The opening chapter models the way that these shifts in perspective create the ominous mood of the novel. It consists of two scenes. In the first a gangster named Popeye watches a man drinking from a spring, and then the man at the spring notices Popeye's reflection in the water. Horace Benbow introduces himself, and they stare at each other for two hours, after which Popeye virtually forces him to accompany him to the "stark square bulk" of a nearby house (7). In the second a former prostitute describes the "crimps and spungs and feebs" who live in the house, in response to which Popeye taunts her, and she calls him "a bastard" (9–10). Wrong-footed in the woods with Horace, Popeye reasserts himself in the house by berating Ruby, the prostitute. The opening thus establishes images and themes of voyeurism and abuse that will recur throughout the novel. For example, Chapter 4 introduces Temple Drake by showing the townspeople and college students watching her, "a snatched coat under her arm and her long legs blonde with running" until she gets into a man's waiting car (28). She looks as if she is in control of her life, going when and where she pleases. At the end of the short chapter, however, her drunken date has crashed their car at the very bootlegging establishment that so recently hosted Horace. The crash "seemed to her to be the logical and disastrous end to the train of circumstance in which she had become involved"; Faulkner stays in her perspective until its end, "her mouth open upon a soundless wail behind her lost breath" as she sees the "feeb" Tommy and Popeye (38–9). She is the victim whom no one hears scream.

The sense of inevitable doom that pervades the beginning of *Sanctuary* only grows as the novel continues and Temple spends a long and terrified night in the Old Frenchman place. Temple's sex appeal and youth mark her as prey to the bootleggers. Van makes an obvious pass at her; Lee Goodwin punishes Van for this, which makes Ruby think he wants her, too; Popeye lurks. Only Tommy has any real sympathy for the "Pore little critter": "Durn them fellers," he thinks (68, 70). Yet even in his sympathy he, too, assumes the role of voyeur, watching Temple through a window. Faulkner uses that combination of kind impulses and sexual obsession to create discomfort and foreboding in his readers. Temple "looked quite small, her very attitude an outrage to muscle and tissue of more than seventeen and more compatible with eight or ten, her elbows close to her sides, her face turned toward the door against which a chair was wedged" (69). Tiny and vulnerable to anyone on the place, Temple obsessively organizes the room and her clothing in order to exert some sort of control over her situation, but her shivering gives her fear away: "The voices had got quiet for a moment and in the silence Tommy could hear a faint, steady chatter of the shucks inside the mattress where Temple lay, her hands crossed on her breast and her legs straight and close and decorous, like an effigy on an ancient tomb" (71). In addition to the sliding narrative perspective, Faulkner retells certain scenes from different points of view. The narrative replays through other eyes, as it does when Ruby and Tommy watch Popeye enter Temple's room and stand next to her bed (80–1). They see nothing in the dark, so neither do we. But when Temple describes the moment later in the novel, we learn that Popeye was not just standing by the bed that night. He was moving his hand down the front of her barely clothed body, and in her terror the moment expanded; it takes her five pages to explain the successive stages of her fear and the mental contortions she performed to try to contain it (215–21).

Because of the way he manipulates his narration, Faulkner can obscure key elements of the plot and spring them later. Popeye's murder of Tommy, for instance, occurs only in Temple's perspective, but at the moment she was concerned only about the threat that Popeye posed to her:

> To Temple, sitting in the cottonseed-hulls and the corncobs, the sound was no louder than the striking of a match: a short, minor sound shutting down upon the scene, the instant, with a profound finality, completely isolating it, and she sat there, her legs straight before her, her hands limp and palm-up on her lap, looking at Popeye's tight back and the ridges of his coat across the shoulders as he leaned out the door, the pistol behind him, against his flank, wisping thinly along his leg.
>
> He turned and looked at her. He waggled the pistol slightly and put it back in his coat, then he walked toward her. Moving, he made no sound at all; the released door either; it was as though sound and silence had become inverted. She could hear silence in a thick rustling as he moved toward her through it, thrusting it aside, and she began to say Something is going to happen to me.   (102)

Faulkner looks away from Temple to Ruby, who sees Temple and Popeye pass in a car and thinks that her face looks "like a small, dead-colored mask drawn past her on a string and then away" (104). Something has indeed happened to Temple, but exactly what remains unclear while Faulkner turns his attention to the man who will soon defend Lee Goodwin against a charge of murder.

Horace met Popeye at the spring in the novel's opening chapter, having just left his wife, and became slightly acquainted with Lee and Ruby later in the evening. He takes up Lee's case out of a combination of pity for Ruby and the baby, and because Lee says he did not kill Tommy, and he seems to keep on it because doing so for "a street-walker, a murderer's woman" makes his self-righteous sister Narcissa so angry (117). Lee will not confess; neither will he implicate Popeye. The impasse is relieved slightly when Ruby tells Horace about Temple's presence at the Old Frenchman place on the day of the murder, and Faulkner then rewinds time to the moments after Ruby saw Temple and Popeye on the road. Sexually violated, Temple watches the same land she traveled "flee backward," much as Faulkner has fled backward in his narrative (137). Popeye takes Temple to Miss Reba's whorehouse in Memphis, where she suffers first the trauma of a gynecological examination and then a second visit from Popeye, "his face wrung above his absent chin, his bluish lips protruding as though he were blowing on hot soup, making a high whinnying sound like a horse" (159). So begins Temple's life as Popeye's mistress. Horace spends the rest of the novel trying to find Temple as a witness for Lee. When he does, Temple testifies that Lee did indeed shoot Tommy. Then the district attorney holds "the stained corncob before her eyes" and "The room sighed, a long hissing breath" – voyeurs all, who have already heard "this horrible, this unbelievable, story which this young girl has told" and "heard the doctor's testimony" and so participated in yet another violation of Temple Drake (288).

Temple's reasons for perjuring herself might include fear of reprisal from Popeye. It must be noted, however, that during her stay at Miss Reba's Temple has developed a definite taste for gin, cigarettes, and sex. She has two lovers, the impotent Popeye and the substitute stud he has procured for her, and at one point she fears that Popeye has killed Red "already" and "she sat in a floating swoon of agonised sorrow and erotic longing, thinking of Red's body, watching her hand holding the empty bottle over the glass" (237). This Temple Drake might well not want the full story of her life in Memphis to emerge in her hometown, and she certainly understands the power wielded there by her father the judge and her four brothers. When Judge Drake removes his daughter from the witness stand and courtroom, the audience cannot take its eyes off her: "the girl could be seen shrunk against the wall just inside the door, her body arched again. She appeared to be clinging there, then the five bodies hid her again and again in a close body the group passed through the door and disappeared." Then, as it did during her testimony, "The room breathed: a buzzing sound like a wind getting up" (290).

No one, then, escapes the mire of the ironically titled *Sanctuary*. Lee is lynched, Horace goes back to his wife, and Popeye is ultimately executed for a crime he did not commit. The novel relies on sliding, voyeuristic narration to produce its primary theme: the sliding, voyeuristic quality of human evil. It also raises the question of what evil is. Horace, for one, thinks that "there's a corruption about even looking upon evil, even by accident; you cannot haggle, traffic, with putrefaction" (129), yet he does exactly that at every turn in the novel. During the night that he interviews Temple at Miss Reba's, he never grasps the simple and obvious fact that she has been raped, but we do. We cringe as we hear her recalled wish for a chastity belt with a spike on it: "I'd jab it all the way through him . . . I didn't know it was going to be just the other way" (218). Horace wants her to talk only about the murder, what he thinks of as "the crime itself" (215). Temple's story so affects him emotionally, however, that after he hears it and looks at the photograph of his stepdaughter of about the same age, he vomits uncontrollably and then, exhausted, merges imaginatively with the violated Temple. The "invitation and voluptuous promise and secret affirmation" in Belle's photograph makes him hear "the shucks set up a furious uproar beneath her thighs"; he becomes a young woman propelled beyond earth to "an interval in which she could swing faintly and lazily in nothingness filled with pale, myriad points of light" (223). As the trap door of the gallows springs open for Popeye, and Temple closes her compact mirror on the image of her "face in miniature sullen and discontented and sad" (317), *Sanctuary* slams shut.

Light in August (1932)

The first six chapters of *Light in August* contain the novel's entire storyline in miniature. A much more conventionally narrated novel than any that precede it, the book develops primarily with flashbacks to explain how its characters came to converge on Jefferson during this life-changing week of August. The main characters tend to fall into one of three constellations, although some overlap occurs at significant points. In the first three chapters we meet Lena Grove, a pregnant and unmarried woman on the road in search of her fugitive boyfriend; Byron Bunch, a mill worker; and Reverend Gail Hightower, removed from his ministry and disgraced in the town. Byron's introduction begins with what he "knows" about a man calling himself Joe Christmas,[11] who it appears has just murdered a local woman named Joanna Burden. Lena, Joe, and Hightower stand at the center of all the action of *Light in August*.

Chapter 6 begins with one of the most famous passages that Faulkner ever wrote, and untangling it offers an important key to the rest of the novel: "Memory believes before knowing remembers." At first glance, this looks like a set of synonyms, but reading further reveals that Faulkner is drawing fine distinctions between these nouns and verbs: "Believes longer than recollects, longer than knowing even wonders," the narrator continues. The person so described "Knows remembers believes" this:

> a corridor in a big long garbled cold echoing building of dark red brick sootbleakened by more chimneys than its own, set in a grassless cinderstrewnpacked compound surrounded by smoking factory purlieus and enclosed by a ten foot steel-and-wire fence like a penitentiary or a zoo, where in random erratic surges, with sparrowlike childtrebling, orphans in identical and uniform blue denim in and out of remembering but in knowing constant as the bleak walls, the bleak windows where in rain soot from the yearly adjacenting chimneys streaked like black tears.   (119)

Memory thus emerges as an unexamined, usually unconscious collection of lived experience, while knowing plays a more active, deliberate role in an individual's life. This passage begins an extended flashback that will explain the events in the orphan Joe Christmas's life that have formed the identity of the man known so casually by Byron Bunch. Like Faulkner's newly minted vocabulary words in the passage above, Joe's identity has been produced by moments of intense and often contradictory experience packed together. The first of these happened when at the age of five he overheard the orphanage's dietician having sex with one of its doctors. She discovered Joe in her closet, vomiting from having eaten too much of her toothpaste in the quiet dark while he waited for the adults to leave: "In the rife, pinkwomansmelling obscurity behind the curtain he squatted, pinkfoamed, listening to his insides, waiting with astonished fatalism for what was about to happen to him. Then it happened. He said to himself with complete and passive surrender: 'Well, here I am'" (122). Thus he acquires at the beginning of his conscious life the fatalism and belief that mark him as an adult in the days before Joanna Burden's death: "he believed with calm paradox that he was the volitionless servant of the fatality in which he believed that he did not believe. He was saying to himself *I had to do it* already in the past tense" (280).

That fatalism joins in Joe with the child's belief in the natural order of crime and punishment: "he believed that he was the one taken in sin and was being tortured with punishment deferred" (123). In a pattern that recurs in Joe's life, his ultimate punishment from the dietician appears as racial punishment. She calls him a "nigger bastard" and makes plans to have him transferred to the "nigger orphanage" (122, 125, 129), but before she can do so the matron places him with the McEachern family. When Joe makes mistakes there, he gets from his adoptive father the swift punishment he understands and from Mrs McEachern the secretive behavior he got from the dietician. Thus begins a set of connections in Joe's memory that believes "men" behave one way, "women" in unpredictably other ways. His first experiences with sex and love reinforce this notion, and his affair with Joanna Burden begins and ends as it does because of that apparently unbreakable chain of associations of men with light, power, and punishment and women with secrecy, darkness, food, and nausea. After his near-coupling with a young black girl, Joe beats her, "enclosed by the womanshenegro and the haste," and fights with other boys until "There was no She at all now. They just fought; it was as if a wind had blown among them, hard and clean" (157).

Throughout his life, Joe cannot choose between the racial associations decreed by those personal ones; they are the racial beliefs at the very core of his memory, to use the term invoked at the beginning of Chapter 6. When he tells his first sweetheart of his racial background, she doubts him, and he replies, "I dont know. I believe I have" (197). When he tells Joanna Burden the same thing, she says, "How do you know that?" and he says, "I dont know it . . . If I'm not, damned if I haven't wasted a lot of time" (254). Indeed, he has: he has tried to live in both the black and the white worlds and never fit in either, and his culture will not allow him to live in both, or in the white one if he is even partially – or even perceived as – black. Lucas Burch, the father of Lena's baby, can deflect suspicion from himself in the matter of Joanna's murder merely by saying, "That's right . . . Go on. Accuse me. Accuse the white man that's trying to help you with what he knows. Accuse the white man and let the nigger go free" (97). As Byron says, "It's like he knew he had them then" (98). At the very center of *Light in August*, Joe and Joanna sit on his bed, talking, at a turning point in their relationship. Joanna describes her family's history of racial attitudes and the contorted form their abolitionism took when it came her father's turn to pass them to her. He took her at the age of four to the graves of her grandfather and brother and told her that they were "murdered not by one white man but by the curse which God put on a whole race before your grandfather or your brother or me or you were even thought of. A race doomed and cursed to be forever and ever a part of the white race's doom and curse for its sins" (252). After this, little Joanna began to see black people differently:

> "But after that I seemed to see them for the first time not as people, but as a thing, a shadow in which I lived, we lived, all white people, all other people. I thought of all the children coming forever and ever into the world, white, with the black shadow already falling upon them before they drew breath. And I seemed to see the black shadow in the shape of a cross. And it seemed like the white babies were struggling, even before they drew breath, to escape the shadow that was not only upon them but beneath them too, flung out like their arms were flung out, as if they were nailed to the cross . . . I couldn't tell then whether I saw it or dreamed it. But it was terrible to me. I cried at night. At last I told father, tried to tell him. What I wanted to tell him was that I must escape, get away from under the shadow, or I would die. 'You cannot,' he said. 'You must struggle, rise. But in order to rise, you must raise the shadow with you. But you can never lift it to your level.'"   (253)

Her father taught her to see black people "not as a people, but as a thing" that she could "never lift" to her "level," and this pathology takes shape in Joanna's mind as the central metaphor of the Christianity that her father practices. With the locked Bible and open catechism in the McEachern parlor (146–7) and Joanna's cross of cursed babies, Faulkner could not offer a clearer indictment of any ideology that reduces people to objects.

Connections abound in this novel between religion, sexuality, race, and gender, with each influencing the other in often unsettling ways. For example, Joe believes that at eight years old he "*became a man*" by resisting McEachern's command to recite the catechism (146); less clear to him is the equally important fact that later that night he also ate the food brought to him by his adoptive mother "like a savage, like a dog" (155). The community comes to look at Joanna's body and her burning house to see "a crime committed not by a negro but by Negro, and who knew, believed, and hoped that she had been ravished too: at least once before her throat was cut and at least once afterward" (288). In the final phase of their relationship, Joanna begins to pray for Joe and to demand that he pray as well, which terrifies him: "As he passed the bed he would look down at the floor beside it and it would seem to him that he could distinguish the prints of knees and he would jerk his eyes away as if it were death that they had looked at" (279). Their battles in this phase produce the only children that either will ever have, as "they would stand for a while longer in the quiet dusk peopled, as though from their loins, by a myriad ghosts of dead sins and delights, looking at one another's still and fading face, weary, spent, and indomitable" (279). In the crazy figure of old Doc Hines, who tells the story of Joe speaking to a black groundskeeper at the orphanage, these issues poignantly coalesce:

> "he says 'I aint a nigger' and the nigger says 'You are worse than that. You dont know what you are. And more than that, you wont never know. You'll live and you'll die and you wont never know' and he says 'God aint no nigger' and the nigger says 'I reckon you ought to know what God is, because dont nobody but God know what you is.' But God wasn't there to say."   (384)

Indeed, God is not there to say. These mortals have to figure things out for themselves.

Reverend Gail Hightower thinks he has done that. He came to Jefferson as a young man with a new wife, to take up the ministry of the local Presbyterian church, because of the stories he heard in childhood of his grandfather's death in the town during the Civil War. His obsession estranged his wife from him, and she died in questionable circumstances in a Memphis hotel, after which his congregation abandoned him. Jefferson has used him as a scapegoat ever since. During the present time of *Light in August*, visited only by Byron Bunch, Hightower spends every evening between dusk and dark sitting in his study window and imagining his grandfather's glorious ride through the streets. Byron brings the news of Joanna's murder to Hightower and soon has even more surprising news: a young pregnant woman has just arrived in Jefferson looking for someone named Lucas Burch. Instead, she found Bunch, who then "fell in love contrary to all the tradition of his austere and jealous country raising which demands in the object physical inviolability" (49). Byron enlists himself as Lena's support system and Hightower as his confidant, and an unlikely combination of characters thus challenges the deterministic portrait of human fate as represented in the life of Joe Christmas. Joe's life has been to him a "street which was to run for fifteen years" (223), a "circle" he could never escape. Hightower's life has come to rest beside the street in town. Lena's story also begins on a road, in the very first sentence of the novel: "Sitting beside the road, watching the wagon mount the hill toward her, Lena thinks, 'I have come from Alabama: a fur piece. All the way from Alabama a-walking. A fur piece'" (30). The end of the novel finds Lena still traveling, this time with her baby and Byron Bunch in tow: "My, my," she says, "A body does get around. Here we aint been coming from Alabama but two months, and now it's already Tennessee" (507). Not only does she live and bring life into the world, but she also follows her own path right out of the book. Lena seems as well to bring out the best in a xenophobic and racist community within which the men and women generally fail to understand one another. When Hightower actually takes time to talk with Lena, her candor and obvious affection for Byron cut right through the stereotype he had held of her as the pregnant woman in search of a husband, any husband. As she waits for Byron to bring Lucas to her, Lena tells Hightower that Byron has proposed marriage and that she has refused him. "This morning about ten oclock he came back," she says, "and he went away. He just stood there, and he went away":

> While he watches her with that despair of all men in the presence of
> female tears, she begins to cry. She sits upright, the child at her breast,
> crying, not loud and not hard, but with a patient and hopeless
> abjectness, not hiding her face. "And you worry me about if I said No or
> not and I already said No and you worry me and worry me and now he
> is already gone. I will never see him again." And he sits there, and she
> bows her head at last, and he rises and stands over her with his hand on
> her bowed head, thinking *Thank God, God help me. Thank God, God
> help me.* (412–13)

"Thank God," perhaps for Lena's decency, maybe for Byron's absence, "God help me" because Hightower stands on a dangerous new precipice from which to view his own life.

He senses this when he mentally thanks Byron for "all he has done for me," "given, restored to me," but the narrator tempers that sense of peace with a warning that just delivering Lena's baby "is not all. There is one thing more reserved for him" (414). That one thing is to be in Percy Grimm's way when he and his gang chase Joe Christmas into Hightower's kitchen and shoot and castrate him, and "upon that black blast the man seemed to rise soaring into their memories forever and ever" (465). In one day Hightower sees the beginning and the ending of human life, and the birth and death act as prompts for the realization of his guilt in his wife's unhappy life and death. He fears this realization: "*I dont want to think this. I must not think this. I dare not think this*" (490). But think it he does: "if I am my dead grandfather on the instant of his death, then my wife, his grandson's wife . . . the debaucher and murderer of my grandson's wife, since I could neither let my grandson live or die" (491). In a beautiful evocation of the novel's title, Faulkner describes Hightower's dying vision:

> In the lambent suspension of August into which night is about to fully come, it seems to engender and surround itself with a faint glow like a halo. The halo is full of faces. The faces are not shaped with suffering, not shaped with anything: not horror, pain, not even reproach. They are peaceful, as though they have escaped into an apotheosis; his own is among them.

The faces include Joe Christmas's "two faces which seem to strive . . . in turn to free themselves one from the other" and Percy Grimm's, and then "some ultimate dammed flood within him breaks and rushes away" (492). Having so recently reentered life, Reverend Gail Hightower reluctantly leaves it. His story connects Lena's to Joe's, and theirs make his complete. When the traveling salesman takes Byron, Lena, and her son into Alabama, the composite stories of *Light in August* move toward a future.

Pylon (1935)

Faulkner had a lifelong fascination with airplanes and pilots. He wrote about them in his first published story, "Landing in Luck," in *Soldiers' Pay*, his first novel, and in some of his best short fiction. In February 1934 Faulkner began a novel that he called *Dark House*, using the title he originally intended for *Light in August*. Also in that year he attended the opening of a new airport in New Orleans, Louisiana, and spent a great deal of time in the company of a reporter writing up the event for the New Orleans *Item* (Blotner 327–8). More than twenty years later, he would claim that he wrote *Pylon* "because I'd got in trouble with *Absalom, Absalom!* and I had to get away from it for a while" (*FIU* 36). One of the five of his novels set outside Yoknapatawpha County, *Pylon* takes place during the opening of a new airport in the fictional New Valois, Franciana, and focuses on a young, unnamed reporter's fascination with two barnstorming pilots, their shared lover, her son, and a mechanic named Jiggs. As he did in *Soldiers' Pay* and *Mosquitoes*, Faulkner used the work of his great modernist predecessors in his text; but he did not do so in order to show off or to use a kind of shorthand for his own ideas. Rather, he subordinated those models to the concerns of *Pylon*, which examines above all else the vexed condition of humanity in a modern age, at the brink of an era when the machine would come to fly the man, at the expense to the latter of his soul.

At first intrigued by the sexual freedom of Roger Shumann's unconventional family, the reporter babbles what he knows so far to his editor, Hagood, who says, "I think you ought to write it."[12] The reporter's response reveals him as a novelist *manqué*:

> "Go home and . . . Home, where I wont be dis – where I can – O pal o pal o pal! Chief, where have I been all your life or where have you been all mine?"
>   "Yes," the editor said. He had not moved. "Go home and lock yourself in and throw the key out the window and write it." He watched the gaunt ecstatic face before him in the dim corpseglare of the green shade. "And then set fire to the room." The reporter's face sank slowly back, like a Halloween mask on a boy's stick being slowly withdrawn. Then for a long time too he did not move save for a faint working of the lips as if he were tasting something either very good or very bad. Then he rose slowly, the editor watching him; he seemed to collect and visibly reassemble himself bone by bone and socket by socket.   (47)

His editor makes matters explicit:

> "The people who own this paper or direct its policies or anyway who pay the salaries, fortunately or unfortunately I shant attempt to say, have no Lewises or Hemingways or even Tchekovs on the staff: one very good reason doubtless being that they do not want them, since what they want is not fiction, not even Nobel Prize fiction, but news."   (47–8)

It does not stretch the text of *Pylon* to see it, among other things, as a representation of one artist having to earn his way in the world as a hack writer.

The editor reminds him that

> "what I am paying you to bring back here is not what you think about somebody out there nor what you heard about somebody out there nor even what you saw: I expect you to come in here tomorrow night with an accurate account of everything that occurs out there tomorrow that creates any reaction excitement or irritation on any human retina."   (48)

That is his definition of news, and the rest of the novel consists of the reporter pursuing the Shumann group precisely in order to find out the things his editor tells him to ignore. Faulkner organizes that quest according to the literary signposts offered by Shakespeare and T. S. Eliot; three of the chapters, for instance, bear the titles "Tomorrow," "And Tomorrow," and "The Love Song of J. A. Prufrock." Like the title character of the latter poem, the reporter does not "dare" do more than observe the life of the fliers. Like Macbeth, with Faulkner using the kinds of neologisms he learned to make from Joyce and perfected in *Light in August*, the reporter feels the futility of his time as he thinks of his city:

> It would be there, the eternal smell of the coffee the sugar the hemp
> sweating slow iron plates above the forked deliberate brown water
> and lost lost lost all ultimate blue of latitude and horizon; the hot
> rain gutterfull plaiting the eaten heads of shrimp; the ten thousand
> inescapable mornings wherein ten thousand airplants swinging
> stippleprop the soft scrofulous soaring of sweating brick and ten
> thousand pairs of splayed brown hired Leonorafeet tigerbarred by
> jaloused armistice with the invincible sun: the thin black coffee, the
> myriad fish stewed in a myriad oil – tomorrow and tomorrow and
> tomorrow; not only not to hope, not even to wait: just to endure.
>
> (291–2)

The novel ends with three of the reporter's manuscript fragments about Roger Shumann's death and Laverne Shumann's departure. The first, edited together from the trash by a copy boy, describes a romantic competition between Shumann and Death, marked by "the Last Checkered Flag" and "his Last Pylon" around which Shumann flew in that contest (323). The second the reporter has left for his editor, and it sarcastically describes the dropping of a memorial wreath by incompetent pilots in an inferior airplane "since they were precision pilots and so did not miss the entire lake" (324). The third is a handwritten note from the reporter, promising to go on a drunken tear because "*I guess this is what you want you bastard*" – the news of "reaction excitement or irritation on any human retina" that is "news" in the modern age.

Absalom, Absalom! (1936)

When the editor Hagood in *Pylon* tells his reporter not to write about "what you think about somebody out there nor what you heard about somebody out there nor even what you saw," he could be describing the very subject matter and narrative process of *Absalom, Absalom!* Faulkner's ninth published novel, arguably his most complex, contains very few of what Hagood would call facts and almost no "news." Put simply, one day late in the Civil War, a man named Henry Sutpen shot a man named Charles Bon at the gates of the plantation built by Henry's father, Thomas. Henry had a white sister, Judith, and a black half-sister, Clytie. Young Quentin Compson grows up hearing the story, and one day in September nearly forty-five years later, he hears part of it firsthand from Rosa Coldfield. Later that night, he takes Rosa to the old plantation house, and there they find Henry Sutpen, but before they can bring an ambulance, Clytie burns the house down. The next January, Rosa dies, and Quentin tells the Sutpen story to his Canadian roommate, Shreve, in their dorm room at Harvard. Chapters 1 through 5 occur one evening in Jefferson in September 1909, Chapters 6 through 9 one evening in January 1910.

Those narrative facts come nowhere near explaining why *Absalom, Absalom!* continues to frustrate and fascinate readers. Just as Quentin, his father and grandfather before him, and Shreve turn over the facts of the Sutpen story, we return to this novel for reasons that say much about us. To some readers, it perfectly illustrates southern history. To some, it explains American race relations. To others, it fills in some reasons for Quentin Compson's suicide in *The Sound and the Fury*, and to still others it is a shining gem of twentieth-century literary modernism. In any case, the novel contains some of Faulkner's most demanding prose. Nowhere in his work is it more tempting and least rewarding to go backward in the reading process in the hope that something you missed will suddenly come clear. One metaphor later in the novel gives a clue as to how to read it successfully, though, and it appears as Quentin muses on Shreve's comment that they have both begun to sound like Quentin's father:

> *Maybe nothing ever happens once and is finished. Maybe happen is never once but like ripples maybe on water after the pebble sinks, the ripples moving on, spreading, the pool attached by a narrow umbilical water-cord to the next pool which the first pool feeds, has fed, did feed, let this second pool contain a different temperature of water, a different molecularity of having seen, felt, remembered, reflect in a different tone the infinite unchanging sky, it doesn't matter: that pebble's watery echo whose fall it did not even see moves across its surface too at the original ripple-space, to the old ineradicable rhythm.*[13]

Things in this novel will never happen once and be finished. Chapters 3 and 4, for example, work their way to the same point in the story and even end with the same character speaking the same words (69, 106). Faulkner wants to examine how stories evolve and what keeps them alive over time – and, not incidentally in the process, what functions they serve in the world. Like the pebble dropped into a pool, whose ripples spread into other pools unaware of that first stone, events in the world of this novel set in motion other events and then disappear. Faulkner's dense prose reflects that aesthetic.

Absalom, Absalom! opens in a hot, airless room in an old house with an old woman talking in a "grim haggard amazed voice" (3) to a young man who would rather be anywhere else. Quentin has answered Miss Rosa Coldfield's "summons," and as he sits in her father's office his attention wanders. He tries to get the facts of the story straight and to figure out exactly why she has called him to the house, and "the getting to it . . . was taking a long time" (8). Rosa has sustained a pitch of outrage against Thomas Sutpen for the past forty-three years, and she rehearses it all in laborious detail for Quentin: "It (the talking, the telling) seemed (to him, to Quentin) to partake of that logic-and reason-flouting quality of a dream which the sleeper knows must have occurred, stillborn and complete, in a second" but which seems real because of "a formal recognition of and acceptance of elapsed and yet-elapsing time as music or a printed tale" (15). Like the said dream, Faulkner's prose, with its parentheticals to clarify references and perspectives, moves its plot ahead by increments. We emerge from the first chapter understanding that Rosa thinks Thomas Sutpen was an "ogre" and that Quentin's resistance to listening to her lessens as she begins to tell the details of Sutpen's semi-barbaric home life.

Chapter 2, also told from Quentin's perspective, recreates Sutpen's arrival in Jefferson and his wedding to Ellen Coldfield, Rosa's older sister. Quentin knows most of this story because "he had been born in and still breathed the same air in which the church bells had rung on that Sunday morning in 1833" when Sutpen appeared in town (23). His grandfather became one of Sutpen's friends, and his father completes Quentin's "day of listening" in 1909 (23) by telling him the story of the wedding as his father told it to him. Early on in the novel, then, we have an emerging series of events told firsthand (by Rosa), secondhand (by Mr Compson, recreating his father's stories), and thirdhand (by Quentin). He will recall all of them as wrapped in the scent of wistaria "which five months later Mr Compson's letter would carry up from Mississippi and over the long iron New England snow and into Quentin's sitting-room at Harvard" (23). Mr Compson takes over as narrator for Chapters 3 and 4. As sources for his version of events, he has a letter from Charles Bon to Judith, his father's stories, and what "the town" knew about the Coldfields and the Sutpens. He tells Quentin about Clytie (Clytemnestra), the child of Thomas Sutpen and one of his original Haitian slaves: "Only I have always liked to believe that he intended to name her Cassandra," he says, "prompted by some pure dramatic economy not only to beget but to designate the presiding augur of his own disaster, and that he just got the name wrong through a mistake natural in a man who must have taught himself to read" (48). The line contains several clues that

Mr Compson is inventing a new version of the Sutpen story and not just passing along unvarnished history. First, he has "always liked to believe" one story of Clytie's naming; second, he cannot imagine that anyone else taught Sutpen how to read. He believes that men and women of that time, "a dead time," were "people too as we are and victims too as we are, but victims of a different circumstance, simpler and therefore, integer for integer, larger, more heroic" than people of the present day, "diffused and scattered creatures drawn blindly limb from limb from a grab bag and assembled, author and victim too of a thousand homicides and a thousand copulations and divorcements" (71). His opinions of people dead and living cannot help but shade his telling of the Sutpen story, and not surprisingly, he is drawn to the figure in it that seems most like himself – Charles Bon.

Mr Compson has long been in possession of a letter from Charles to Judith, written near the end of the war and given by Judith herself to Quentin's grandmother. He passes on Judith's stated reason for giving the letter away: "maybe if you could go to someone, the stranger the better, and give them something . . . at least it would be something just because it would have happened, be remembered" (101). Judith's gesture, coupled with the exhausted cynicism of Charles's letter, has moved Mr Compson to try to imagine what could have caused Henry to kill the man his sister loved. The only thing he can come up with that seems dire enough a cause is a previous marriage, and one to a woman of mixed race – in his view, an octoroon of New Orleans. He imagines Henry as a country bumpkin and Charles as the worldly connoisseur explaining that such women are "Not whores. And not whores because of us, the thousand. We – the thousand, the white men – made them, created and produced them; we even made the laws which declare that one eighth of a specified kind of blood shall outweigh seven eighths of another kind" (91). Mr Compson sees Charles Bon as a white man like himself. He has Charles talk about "us, the white men" who created the courtesans whom he also imagines as "creatures taken at childhood, culled and chosen and raised more carefully than any white girl, any nun, than any blooded mare even, by a person who gives them the unsleeping care and attention which no mother ever gives" and then "raised and trained to fulfill a woman's sole end and purpose: to love, to be beautiful, to divert" (93). He brings his opinions of women and of southern race relations to bear on the Sutpen facts as he knows them, and he despairs of finding their meaning: "It just does not explain. Or perhaps that's it: they dont explain and we are not supposed to know" (80).

When Quentin and Shreve recount the Sutpen facts between them, they produce a very different "reason" for Henry to shoot Charles Bon. To Quentin's father, these heroic "integers" from a "dead time" act out their passions "against that turgid background of a horrible and bloody mischancing of human affairs" – in itself a pretty romanticized account of the Civil War (80). Quentin and Shreve, young men of about Henry's and Charles's age, weave a tale that seems to bear out Mr Compson's belief that "it would not be the first time that youth has taken catastrophe as a direct act of Providence for the sole purpose of solving a personal problem which youth itself could not solve" (95). Mr Compson's story does not move Quentin's imagination, however, until he brings it to the gate where the shooting occurred. Then, "It seemed to Quentin that he could actually see them . . . the two faces calm, the voices not even raised: *Dont you pass the shadow of this branch, Charles;* and *I am going to pass it, Henry"* (105–6). Similarly, when Faulkner picks up Miss Rosa's afternoon monologue, Quentin "could not pass" the moment when she describes Henry charging into Judith's bedroom after shooting Charles. He seizes one of Rosa's details – Judith in her underthings, snatching at her wedding dress to cover herself – as an established fact and imagines the scene that, to him, must necessarily have followed:

> *Now you cant marry him*
> *Why cant I marry him?*
> *Because he's dead*
> *Dead?*
> *Yes. I killed him.*   (139–40)

So taken is he with this image that he "was not even listening" to Rosa: we hear her talk for thirty-one pages, but Quentin does not. Twice he has come to the moment in the Sutpen story that he wants to imagine for himself, and like his father before him and Shreve alongside him at Harvard, he adds to the "facts" in order to make the story satisfy his demands as a listener.

When Shreve helps him with the narrative, *Absalom, Absalom!* becomes even more densely layered because Shreve not only gets new information out of Quentin – like the long story that his grandfather told about Sutpen's "design" for his own life (178–222) – but because he, too, joins in the invention of details that he needs to find the story satisfying. Often Quentin does not want to surrender the narration: "that voice with its tense suffused restrained quality: 'I am telling'" (222); but Shreve takes over anyway: "No," he says once, "you wait. Let me play a while now" (224). And in spite of the fact that Quentin admits that "nobody ever did know if Bon ever knew Sutpen was his father or not" (216), in the story that Quentin and Shreve make, Bon did know that Sutpen was his father and sought to marry Judith in order to force his father's acknowledgment:

> Because he knew exactly what he wanted; it was just the saying of it – the
> physical touch even though in secret, hidden – the living touch of that
> flesh warmed before he was born by the same blood which it had
> bequeathed him to warm his own flesh with, to be bequeathed by him in
> turn to run hot and loud in veins and limbs after that first flesh and then
> his own were dead.   (255)

This Charles Bon wants what the biblical King David gave his estranged son
Absalom, after Absalom led a revolt against him. In spite of that treachery,
when he heard that Absalom was dead, David "went up to the chamber over
the gate, and wept: and as he went, thus he said, O my son Absalom, my son,
my son Absalom! would God I had died for thee, O Absalom, my son, my son!"
(II Samuel 18:33). Thus the title of Faulkner's novel enshrines the Sutpen story
that Quentin and Shreve ultimately create between them.

Faulkner repeatedly calls attention to the deliberately invented characteristics of that story, and in doing so he highlights the continuously evolving
relationship that exists between all good storytellers and their material. For
example, at one point Shreve solves a plot difficulty by imagining a conniv-
ing lawyer who brings together Charles, Charles's mother, and the Sutpens of
Mississippi. As a result of that invention, Quentin and Shreve can actually enter
the story they tell:

> So that now it was not two but four of them riding the two horses
> through the dark over the frozen December ruts of that Christmas eve:
> four of them and then just two – Charles-Shreve and Quentin-Henry . . .
>   . . . [and] four of them who sat in that drawing room of baroque and
> fusty magnificence which Shreve had invented and which was probably
> true enough, while the Haiti-born daughter of the French sugar planter
> and the woman who Sutpen's first father-in-law had told him was a
> Spaniard . . . whom Shreve and Quentin had likewise invented and
> which was likewise probably true enough . . .   (268)

"True enough" describes the realm of verisimilitude rather than of history, and
Faulkner asks readers of this novel to do what Quentin and Shreve do when
they get the details to suit themselves. They lose their own time and space and
enter another:

> Because now neither of them was there. They were both in Carolina
> and the time was forty-six years ago, and it was not even four now but
> compounded still further, since now both of them were Henry Sutpen
> and both of them were Bon, compounded each of both yet either
> neither, smelling the very smoke which had blown and faded away
> forty-six years ago from the *bivouac fires burning in a pine grove, the*

gaunt and ragged men sitting or lying about them, talking not about the
war yet curiously enough (or perhaps not curiously at all) facing the South
where further on in the darkness the pickets stood . . . (280)

The italics signal our entry into that night forty-six years before the evening
in 1910, which we have likewise entered with our two narrators, all of us
"compounded" of one another in the pages of Faulkner's novel.

Were *Absalom, Absalom!* to end with Quentin's and Shreve's vision of Bon's
romantic concern for Judith's feelings after his death, it would resolve rather
easily. Instead, it ends with an exchange that forces a return to the previous
chapters. Shreve has summed up the Sutpen story as though it amounted to
a parable of race in the American South: "You've got one nigger left. One
nigger Sutpen left," and "You still hear him at night sometimes. Dont you?"
(302). He implies that the miscegenation still haunts the white folks and will
continue to do so until "in time the Jim Bonds are going to conquer the western
hemisphere," and then he asks Quentin something that reverberates through
all we have heard: "Now I want you to tell me just one thing more. Why do you
hate the South?" (302–3). Shreve could say these words in earnest, as though
he really wanted a thoughtful answer, or he could say them sarcastically, as
though the response were self-evident. In either case, Quentin's defensiveness
and almost reflexive terror close the novel: "'I dont hate it,' Quentin said,
quickly, at once, immediately; 'I dont hate it,' he said. *I dont hate it* he thought,
panting in the cold air, the iron New England dark: *I dont. I dont! I dont hate*
it! I dont hate it!" (303).

The way that we decide to read these lines both determines and is determined
by what we would make of the stories and narrators that precede them. Should
we read like Rosa Coldfield, we will see a story of stifled girlhood and denied
romantic ambition. Should we read like Mr Compson, we will find various sets
of characters all doomed to death and oblivion. Should we read like Quentin,
we will resist revisiting the stories of our own past, but we will be drawn against
our volition back into them: "*I am going to have to hear it all over again I am*
already hearing it all over again I am listening to it all over again I shall have to
never listen to anything else but this again forever" (222). This last chapter in the
Sutpen story also brings out, after forty-six years, a new fact: Henry Sutpen,
still alive, came back to Sutpen's Hundred "*To die*," and Quentin helped to
discover this on the night in September that he took Rosa Coldfield to the old
house. He is not to lose the image of "the wasted yellow face with closed, almost
transparent eyelids on the pillow, the wasted hands crossed on the breast as if
he were already a corpse"; "waking or sleeping it was the same and would be the
same forever as long as he lived" (298). With Shreve busy constructing a vision

of the South that can take the place of "'something my people haven't got'" (289), Quentin remains stuck with the living memory of touching the Sutpen story firsthand, in the person of its surviving son – the son whose absence was mourned, the son whose father claimed him.

The Unvanquished (1938)

In the mid-1930s, during a hiatus from work on *Absalom, Absalom!*, Faulkner published a series of stories in the *Saturday Evening Post* and *Scribner's* magazines about Bayard Sartoris's childhood during the Civil War and Reconstruction. This was the Old Bayard of *Flags in the Dust/Sartoris*, Faulkner's first novel set in Yoknapatawpha County. Because Sartoris family members also appear in some of Faulkner's short fiction, criticism on *The Unvanquished* often reads intertextually to try to discover Faulkner's attitudes toward the aristocratic ante- and postbellum class rather than look at the specifics of what happens in this book. And because it is infinitely more accessible than *Absalom* or *Light in August*, critics have tended to take it less seriously and devoted less attention to explicating it than those other two novels so deeply concerned with the Civil War. Indeed, teachers often recommend *The Unvanquished* as a good novel with which to begin reading Faulkner.

Faulkner revised the first six chapters of the novel (the previously published stories) and added a seventh, "An Odor of Verbena," to finish rounding the material into a whole. The plot traces Bayard's life from 1862, when as a twelve-year-old he recreates Civil War battlefields, to 1874, when as a 24-year-old he studies law. His best friend, the slave boy Ringo, is his constant companion as the South loses the war, the Sartoris family struggles through Reconstruction, and Bayard's father dies at the hands of a former business partner. A Miss Rosa figures prominently in this novel, as one does in *Absalom, Absalom!* This time, though, it is the tough Miss Rosa Millard, Bayard's "Granny," who keeps order on the plantation during the war and devises a scheme to get the Yankees to pay her for their own stolen livestock. In order to do this, she must make business alliances with shady characters such as Ab Snopes and the renegade Grumby, who eventually kills her. Bayard and Ringo avenge her death; John Sartoris comes home from the war and, under duress, marries his cousin Drusilla, who lost her fiancé and her interest in femininity during the war. Together, John and Drusilla foil Jefferson's first, hopelessly corrupt, Reconstruction election. In the book's final chapter, when Bayard refuses to kill the man who killed his father, the old order of Sartoris authority, based on violence and vengeance, passes.

As this summary suggests, *The Unvanquished* is episodic, and this quality of its construction is precisely Faulkner's point: the book is a series of important episodes in the formation of a boy's character. Less social history than *Bildungsroman*, the book represents Bayard's movement from worshipping his father to understanding him as a man and, establishing himself as an adult in the process, learning to mourn his passing. At first, Bayard smells on John Sartoris "that odor in his clothes and beard too which I believed was the smell of powder and glory, the elected victorious."[14] In a phrase that anticipates his own maturation, though, he adds, "but know better now: know now to have been only the will to endure, a sardonic and even humorous declining of self-delusion which is not even kin to that optimism which believes that that which is about to happen to us can possibly be the worst which we can suffer" (10). He learns that he can want to kill, and that he can do so. When he and Ringo track down Granny's killer, at first Bayard cannot move;

> then my arm began to come up with the pistol and he turned and
> ran. He shouldn't have tried to run from us in boots. Or maybe that
> made no difference either, because now my arm had come up and now
> I could see Grumby's back (he didn't scream, he never made a sound)
> and the pistol both at the same time and the pistol was level and steady
> as a rock. (183)

At this point he is truly "John Sartoris' boy" (186), and even though he recognizes some realities of the adult world, he still has some growing up to do. For instance, he understands the injustice of the gender politics that force his father and Drusilla to marry; he has to run from the room when he sees the trap close on her and "heard the light sharp sound when Drusilla's head went down between her flungout arms on the table" (203). He also comes to question the kind of "dream" that requires the slaughter of human beings (223–4). When he hears the news of his father's murder, he takes a course of action he has premeditated: "*At least this will be my chance to find out if I am what I think I am or if I just hope; if I am going to do what I have taught myself is right or if I am just going to wish I were*" (215). Bayard does indeed learn that he has become the man he wished to be when he faces his father's killer unarmed, and Faulkner's invocation of the Sutpen story from *Absalom, Absalom!* brings that important strand of *The Unvanquished*'s lessons about adulthood into focus. Sutpen, Bayard says, "came back home and set out singlehanded to rebuild his plantation," "to rebuild the place like it used to be" (222). John Sartoris, on the other hand, built toward the future but could not outrun his violent past: "I acted as the land and the time demanded," he says, "But now the land and the time too are changing," and that world is Bayard's to navigate, for himself and his family (231). And that man in his coffin, "the nose, the hair, the eyelids closed over the intolerance" (236), Bayard mourns as Thomas Sutpen did no man, with "illimitable grief and regret" (236): "I went to sleep almost before I had stopped thinking. I slept for almost five hours and I didn't dream anything at all yet I waked myself up crying, crying too hard to stop it" (252). The fact that he can love and mourn and still assert his own principles allows Bayard to believe that his father "would always be there; maybe what Drusilla meant by his dream was not something which he possessed but something which he had bequeathed us which we could never forget, which would even assume the corporeal shape of him whenever any of us, black or white, closed our eyes" (253). In the world of this novel, dreaming counts as a kind of self-delusion, whether done by the migrating slaves at the river or John Sartoris or Drusilla Hawk. Memory, on the other hand, can accept both the reality of the delusion and the essential worth of the flawed men and women who suffer from it. Memory can grieve, and from grief in the living springs the only kind of immortality that a human might certainly know.

If I Forget Thee, Jerusalem (*The Wild Palms*) (1939)

Memory and grief saturate the pages of Faulkner's eleventh novel, particularly in the primary plot entitled "The Wild Palms." In that story a medical intern named Harry Wilbourne meets Charlotte Rittenmeyer, the married mother of two girls and artist *manqué*, and runs away with her to try to live life as "all honeymoon, always."[15] Charlotte uses that phrase to exhort Harry to believe, as she does, in romantic love expressed sexually: "Either heaven, or hell: no comfortable safe peaceful purgatory between for you and me to wait in until good behavior or forbearance or shame or repentance overtakes us." Love, she says, "doesn't die. It just leaves you, goes away, if you are not good enough, worthy enough. It doesn't die; you're the one that dies" (71). Their story begins in 1937 on the Mississippi Gulf Coast, with Charlotte very ill and Harry in search of a doctor. Told in flashback over five chapters, "The Wild Palms" alternates with five chapters of "Old Man," the story of a convict battling the Great Flood of 1927. The plots do not seem to have very much in common, and the novel is one of five not set in Yoknapatawpha County, so readers early and late have had trouble coming to terms with the book's place in Faulkner's career. Yet it contains some of Faulkner's most well-wrought prose, and reading the alternating stories creates suspense as the book progresses. With *The Unvanquished* and this novel, Faulkner seems to have become interested in crafting novels out of discrete episodes rather than alternating points of view, as he did in *The Sound and the Fury* and *As I Lay Dying.* When he talked publicly about the book, he said as much:

> To tell the story I wanted to tell, which was the one of the intern and the woman who gave up her family and husband to run off with him. To tell it like that, somehow or another I had to discover a counterpoint for it, so I invented the other story, its complete antithesis, to use as counterpoint. And I did not write those two stories and then cut one into the other. I wrote them, as you read it, as the chapters. (*LIG* 132)
>
> That was one story – the story of Charlotte Rittenmeyer and Harry Wilbourne, who sacrificed everything for love and then lost that . . . I realized suddenly that something was missing, it needed emphasis, something to lift it like a counterpoint in music. So I wrote on the "Old Man" story until the "Wild Palms" story rose back to pitch. (*LIG* 247)

The alternating plots pull readers through the book in opposite ways. Harry and Charlotte's story begins near its end, and Faulkner piques our curiosity to discover how they have come to this sad place on the coast. The tall convict's story begins at the beginning of the Great Flood and describes his astonishing adventures as he is sent out on its waters to rescue a woman in a tree and a man on a cotton house (65).

We first see Charlotte through the eyes of the doctor who will summon help for her: "the dark-haired woman with queer hard yellow eyes in a face whose skin was drawn thin over prominent cheekbones and a heavy jaw," absorbed in "that complete immobile abstraction from which even pain and terror are absent, in which a living creature seems to listen to and even to watch some one of its own flagging organs, the heart say, the secret irreparable seeping of blood" (5). He overhears her call her companion a "damned" and "bloody bungling bastard" (17, 18); we thus get an early hint that Charlotte's "flagging organs" do not include her heart. Midway through the novel, while working as a doctor at a mine in Utah, Harry performs an abortion – illegal in the United States at that time, and so carrying great risk for the woman, her husband, and Harry. Harry and Charlotte's discussion of this sounds an ominous note:

> "You are afraid?"
> "No. It's nothing. Simple enough. A touch with the blade to let the air in. It's because I – "
> "Women do die of it though."
> "Because the operator was no good. Maybe one in ten thousand. Of course there are no records. It's because I –" (161)

Charlotte soon becomes pregnant, and after trying to avoid performing the abortion she requests, he agrees. But this time he is desperately afraid: the operator is no good, and this woman dies of it.

Harry is sentenced to fifty years of hard labor in the State Penitentiary at Parchman (270), but he gets an unexpected way out of that sentence when Charlotte's husband visits him in jail with a gift of cyanide. Not quite knowing why, Harry rejects the option of suicide, and his story closes as he reasons out his decision. He thinks that he and Charlotte had asked "so little" of life, just to love each other and be let alone; they quit many a job and moved to many a place in search of that goal. He concludes that the memory of love lives in the body itself. Even "*the old meat*" can still love: "*Because if memory exists outside of the flesh it wont be memory because it wont know what it remembers so when she became not then half of memory became not and if I become not then all of remembering will cease to be*" (272–3). When he concludes that "*Between grief and nothing I will take grief,*" he chooses a highly romantic way to view the fact that he himself has erased the "remembering" not only of his lover but of his child. Faulkner offers that caution by way of the final pages of the tall convict's story. He has braved the flood, helped the pregnant woman in the tree to give birth, wrestled alligators with a Cajan business partner, and survived the blowing of the Mississippi River levees in the flood, only to return on purpose to life in "the known, the desired" clothing of a state convict (285). Faulkner plays much of his story for humor, but from the comic language the convict's real distrust of women and fear of the chaotic world that they seem to embody emerge plainly. For example, after the child's birth, he looks at it and thinks, "*And this is all. This is what severed me violently from all I ever knew and did not wish to leave and cast me upon a medium I was born to fear, to fetch up at last in a place I never saw before and where I do not even know where I am*" (194). He gives thanks for the flood's opposite: "it was hard at times to drive a plow through, it sent you spent, weary, and cursing its light-long insatiable demands back to your bunk at sunset at times but it did not snatch you violently out of all familiar knowing and sweep you thrall and impotent for days against any returning" (195). In sum, he wants what he knows, what he can predict: "*All in the world I wanted was just to surrender*" (207). The man does not have Harry's education or vocabulary; Faulkner uses his own elevated diction and complex syntax to reflect the convict's inner state, and that state is as self-delusional as Harry's. He would, like Harry, hide from life and its responsibilities, especially as represented by woman: "Women, shit," he says in the novel's last line (287).

If I Forget Thee, Jerusalem, Faulkner's original title for the novel, was changed by his publishers to *The Wild Palms* in order to highlight Harry and Charlotte's story. Faulkner fought for his original title on the grounds that "it invented itself as a title for the chapter in which Charlotte died and where Wilbourne said 'Between grief and nothing I will take grief' . . . just as 'The Unvanquished' was the title of the story of Granny's struggle between her morality and her children's needs" (*SL* 106). He lost the argument, but the passage in Psalms from which he took his original title makes his case. In exile, "By the rivers of Babylon, there we set down, yea, we wept, when we remembered Zion," the Israelites sang. When asked to sing of their home, they asked, "How shall we sing the Lord's song in a strange land?" and went on to pledge their loyalty to home: "If I forget thee, O Jerusalem, let my right hand forget her cunning. If I do not remember thee, let my tongue cleave to the roof of my mouth; if I prefer not Jerusalem above my chief joy" (Psalm 137:1, 4–6). Harry chooses to remember and live for the memory of his Jerusalem; the tall convict retreats to his own. Sentenced to ten extra years for attempted escape, the tall convict will be in Parchman when Harry gets there to begin serving his sentence. Faulkner therefore asks us to ask about the songs they sing in this strange land, where their exiles really lie, and what paradise they finally achieve.

The Hamlet (1940)

Continuing with experiments in episodic narration, *The Hamlet* marks a return to the conventional, third-person omniscient narrative voice that takes up the plot in a more or less chronological fashion, not unlike *Light in August*. The novel's title lets us know that what follows is a view of a community. This particular one, Frenchman's Bend, lies "Hill-cradled and remote, definite yet without boundaries," home to "Protestants and Democrats and prolific" poorer white folks; "there was not one negro landowner in the entire section. Strange negroes would absolutely refuse to pass through it after dark."[16] Faulkner soon introduces the major players in this part of the world. Will Varner, the area's richest man, has sixteen children; his ninth, Jody, runs his business affairs for him. One day a family named Snopes arrives and rents a farm from the Varners. Soon they learn that the patriarch, Ab, has a reputation as a barn-burner. They receive further news about the Snopeses from the "pleasant, affable, courteous, anecdotal and impenetrable" sewing-machine agent V. K. Ratliff, an itinerant man who "never forgot a name and he knew everyone, man mule and dog, within fifty miles" (14). By the time the first section of the first chapter ends, the oldest Snopes child, Flem, has traded on Jody's fear of his father's reputation to get a position as a clerk in Varner's store. "Aint no benefit in farming," Flem says, "I figure on getting out of it soon as I can" (25). Thus begins his journey away from life as a sharecropper in his father's house – a journey that will take him at the end of the novel to Jefferson, as the acknowledged head of the Snopes clan.

Faulkner organized *The Hamlet* into four named books. "Flem" ends with the title character moving into Varner's house as he continues his march up the Bend's corporate ladder; his character emerges as the compilation of stories that the people know about him. These stories include Ratliff's recollections of Ab's younger days, before he was "soured" by life (29), and an elaborate tale of a goat-trading deal that sets up Ratliff and Flem as rivals in Frenchman's Bend. The latter story introduces two other Snopes, Isaac and Mink, who will play important roles later in the novel. Book 2, "Eula," opens with a description of Will Varner's youngest child, whose "entire appearance suggested some symbology out of the old Dionysic times," "the queen, the matrix" of "anything in which blood ran" (105, 128). Eula becomes pregnant near the end of Book 2, and her parents marry her off to the nearest convenient man – Flem Snopes, right down the hall, who trades the favor for financial incentives from Will, including a long honeymoon in Texas. Faulkner elaborately describes Eula's sex appeal, sometimes for laughs and sometimes in dead earnest, because in showing how much men want her and how they seek to use her, he can show parallels between sexual relationships and commodity deals. Trading goats becomes not so very different from marrying off your daughter. For her and for the community, the stakes turn tragic. The "little lost village, nameless, without grace, forsaken, yet which wombed once by chance and accident one blind seed of the spendthrift Olympian ejaculation and did not even know it" sees its goddess vanish: "a lean, loose-jointed, cotton-socked, shrewd, ruthless old man, the splendid girl with her beautiful masklike face, the froglike creature which barely reached her shoulder, cashing a check, buying a license, taking a train" (164). Ratliff sees in Eula's married face "only another mortal natural enemy of the masculine race" quickly supplanted in his imagination by Flem's tobacco-chewing one. "Eula" ends in Ratliff's vision of Flem tricking the Prince of Hell out of his throne; indeed, "Eula" herself disappears from the novel, known in later chapters only as "Mrs Flem Snopes" (293).

"The Long Summer," Book 3, begins without the newly married couple. A lengthy flashback tells the story of the mentally deficient Isaac "Ike" Snopes's love for and love affair with the landowner Jack Houston's cow. In some of the most melodious prose he ever wrote, Faulkner describes Ike's world with the cow:

> the dawn would be empty, the moment and she would not be, then he would hear her and he would lie drenched in the wet grass, serene and one and indivisible in joy, listening to her approach. He would smell her; the whole mist reeked with her; the same malleate hands of mist which drew along his prone drenched flanks palped her pearled barrel too and shaped them both somewhere in immediate time, already married.   (183)

Such language expresses Ike's emotional life even as it suppresses what he actually does with the cow. We learn that from the reactions of other characters. I. O. Snopes makes matters explicit: "The Snopes name has done held its head up too long in this country to have no such reproaches against it like stock-diddling" (222). The stock-diddling has become a sideshow in the Bend, and Ratliff forces the other Snopeses to shut it down and seek a "cure" for Ike's obsession. The local minister tells them that they must "beef the critter the fellow has done formed the habit with and cook a piece of it and let him eat it" so that "not only the boy's mind but his insides too, the seat of his passion and sin, can have the proof that the partner of his sin is dead" (223–4). The entire episode parodies Eula's marriage to Flem, which happened to keep her family's reputation intact, just as I. O. says that they must pay to cure Ike because "The Snopes name" has "got to be kept pure as a marble monument for your children to grow up under" (226). One financial arrangement damns a woman for the sake of a family name, the other kills for it.

Faulkner continues his representations of relationships between the sexes in the second chapter of "The Long Summer," which traces Jack Houston's marriage to Lucy Pate and Mink Snopes's to the sexually wild daughter of a conscript labor foreman. When Mink kills Houston because of a lawsuit between them, Mink discovers that his remaining life is forever joined to the man he murdered: "he had pulled trigger on an enemy but had only slain a corpse to be hidden"; "I thought that when you killed a man, that finished it, he told himself. But it dont. It just starts then" (242, 269). Book 4, "The Peasants," widens its focus by casting another deal for animals in terms of a contest between the public, male-dominated space of the auction ring with the female-run domestic space of Mrs Littlejohn's boarding house, which sits opposite. All during the auction of the wild Texas ponies, Mrs Littlejohn comes out of the house to do chores, ignoring the doings of the men paying good money for obviously untamable horses. When one of the horses invades her home, "'Get out of here, you son of a bitch,' she said. She struck with the wash-board; it divided neatly on the long mad face and the horse whirled and rushed back up the hall" (335). Over the next few days, the story of the auction starts to take shape as public entertainment, which will turn into communal lore, and finally history. The humor takes center stage, as Ratliff narrates:

> "Maybe there wasn't but one of them things in Mrs Littlejohn's house that night, like Eck says. But it was the biggest drove of just one horse I ever seen. It was in my room and it was on the front porch and I could hear Mrs Littlejohn hitting it over the head with that wash-board in the back yard all at the same time. And still it was missing everybody

> everytime. I reckon that's what that Texas man meant by calling them
> bargains: that a man would need to be powerful unlucky to ever get close
> enough to one of them to get hurt."
>
> . . .
>
> [One listener says]: "I wonder how many Ratliffs that horse thought
> he saw."
> "I dont know," Ratliff said. "But if he saw just half as many of me as I
> saw of him, he was sholy surrounded."   (341, 342)

However, this bantering disappears upon the instant Ratliff seems to get an
admission that Flem Snopes owned the horses and so fleeced the buyers; that
somber change introduces the story of Henry Armstid and his wife, whose
poverty is extreme even in Frenchman's Bend. Nothing would do but that
Henry buy a horse with the money Mrs Armstid earned for her children. Yet
Flem will not admit owning the horses, so he will not refund Mrs Armstid's
money, even though everyone at the auction has seen him take her money
(327). In this way he beats everyone in Frenchman's Bend out of something –
everyone except Ratliff.

Ratliff's comeuppance at Flem's hands happens in the last extended episode
of the novel, in which he and two partners (including the nearly deranged
Henry Armstid) buy the Old Frenchman's place because they believe that Flem
has discovered buried treasure on the property. Ratliff believes in "the stub-
born tale of the money" that Faulkner planted subtly in his initial description of the antebellum house (4), so it takes little effort for Flem to arrange
for Ratliff to witness what he wants to believe. Instead of finding treasure,
however, Flem was burying it; when Ratliff and his partners buy the place,
they cut Flem's last financial tie to Frenchman's Bend. He packs up his newly
arrived family and heads to Jefferson to take up part ownership in the restaur-
ant that Ratliff traded in part for the old house. He leaves *The Hamlet*, then,
having wrung every last bit of profit out of it that he can. A perfect example
of American upward mobility, Flem also embodies the darker side of such
progress. He himself is viciously amoral at best; his home is a sham, and he
leaves others wrecked in his wake. As Armstid digs for the treasure that everyone knows he will not find, the residents of the Bend create the moral of the
story:

> "He's still at it."
> "He's going to kill himself. Well, I dont know as it will be any loss."
> "Not to his wife, anyway."
> "That's a fact. It will save her that trip every day toting food to him.
> That Flem Snopes."

"That's a fact. Wouldn't no other man have done it."

"Couldn't no other man have done it. Anybody might have fooled Henry Armstid. But couldn't nobody but Flem Snopes have fooled Ratliff."

(405)

The novel closes with Flem driving away from the Bend, an image of ominous mobility that sat at the heart of Faulkner's first ideas about the Snopeses and their stories. He began work on this family in the mid-1920s, and although he never published the *Father Abraham* manuscript that contained them, they found their way into nearly every novel he wrote after *Flags in the Dust/Sartoris* and into a great many of his short stories. By December 1938, with *The Unvanquished* in print and *The Wild Palms* at the publishers, he knew that his "Snopes book" would probably take up three separate volumes (*SL* 107). "The Peasants" was the working title for *The Hamlet*. The other two volumes would become *The Town* and *The Mansion*, and as Faulkner predicted to his editor, they describe "the gradual eating-up of Jefferson by Snopes" (*SL* 107). The details of that eating-up, however, would blossom and change in Faulkner's imagination for the next nineteen years.

Go Down, Moses (1942)

Faulkner's publishers released Faulkner's thirteenth novel under the title *Go Down, Moses and Other Stories* because they thought that a collection of short stories would sell better than a novel. Indeed, he had been writing stories about black families on tenant farms and placing them in national magazines, and letters to his editors in 1940 show that he had an interest in revising them into a novel as he had done *The Unvanquished* (*SL* 122, 124, 128). Also like that novel, *Go Down, Moses* uses individual titles rather than chapter numbers to mark its major divisions; and with the exception of "The Bear," these seven chapters can stand alone as short stories. But a novel is a sustained investigation with scope as well as depth in theme, character development, and plot; its various notes combine into chords over the course of its narrative, and in a superb novel those chords depend upon one another for their fullest expression. *Go Down, Moses* achieves just such a symphonic resonance.

"Was" opens the novel by introducing a character who does not even appear in the action of the chapter: "Isaac McCaslin, 'Uncle Ike,' past seventy and nearer eighty than he ever corroborated any more, a widower now and uncle to half a county and father to no one"[17] – and no punctuation mark closes that opening line. It sets up Isaac as a conduit for the story that will come, and we hear next that "this was not something participated in or even seen by himself, but by his elder cousin, McCaslin Edmonds, grandson of Isaac's father's sister and so descended by the distaff, yet notwithstanding the inheritor, and in his time the bequestor, of that which some thought then and some still thought should have been Isaac's" (3). Like the opening lines of *The Sound and the Fury*, these lines make no sense at all until we read nearly all of the rest of the novel, but after we do so, they echo with significance. The story that follows is "out of the old time, the old days" (4), and it traces the comic attempt of Sophonsiba Beauchamp to trap one twin brother into matrimony and the less comic attempt of a slave to visit his sweetheart on the Beauchamp land. Told from nine-year-old McCaslin's point of view, the story achieves its humor from the scrupulous way that Cass records what the adults say and do without understanding the full meaning of what he reports:

> They went into the dining room and ate and Miss Sophonsiba said how seriously now neighbors just a half day's ride apart ought not to go so long as Uncle Buck did, and Uncle Buck said Yessum, and Miss Sophonsiba said Uncle Buck was just a confirmed roving bachelor from the cradle born and this time Uncle Buck even quit chewing and looked and said, Yes, ma'am, he sure was, and born too late at it to ever change now but at least he could thank God no lady would ever have to suffer the misery of living with him and Uncle Buddy, and Miss Sophonsiba said, ah, that maybe Uncle Buck just aint met the woman yet who would not only accept what Uncle Buck was pleased to call misery, but who would make Uncle Buck consider even his freedom a small price to pay, and Uncle Buck said, "Nome. Not yet." (11)

Buck enters Sophonsiba's territory in search of the slave Tomey's Turl, who loves the Beauchamp slave Tennie and runs off a few times a year to see her. The highly ritualized nature of the chase adds to its humor – Buck always has to put on a necktie to go to get Turl, for example – but that humor fades when we realize that Buck chases a man, a man in love, and not a fox. His brother's poker acumen gets him out of this particular trap, but Turl has dealt the cards they play. Hubert "reached out and tilted the lamp-shade, the light moving up Tomey's Turl's arms that were supposed to be black but were not quite white" (28), and when we recall that Hubert "said he wouldn't have that damn white half-McCaslin on his place even as a free gift" (6), the humor of the story fades further. As subsequent stories make clear, Buck is chasing not just a slave but his brother. When we discover that Sophonsiba and Buck are Isaac McCaslin's parents, "Was" becomes exemplary of their courtship: at least once, Sophonsiba caught Buck; and at least once, he did not mind, and the result was Isaac. The initial humor of *Go Down, Moses* dissolves into the irony and paradox of simultaneously loving, trapping, and owning human beings.

Relationships between men and women in this book are all racialized, and all race relations in it are sexualized, as the next two chapters illustrate. The present-time narrative of "The Fire and the Hearth" concerns Lucas Beauchamp's efforts to locate rumored buried treasure. The substance of the story, told in flashback, seeks to explain Lucas's character and pride as a male descendant of Carothers McCaslin. For example, Lucas must negotiate tricky race protocols in order to get a rival bootlegger shut down: "The report would have to come from Edmonds, the white man, because to the sheriff Lucas was just another nigger and both the sheriff and Lucas knew it, although only one of them knew that to Lucas the sheriff was a redneck without any reason for pride in his forbears nor hope for it in his descendants" (43). Yet he believes himself to be of "better men than these" (44), one belonging to "the old time when men black and white were men" (37). Going to see Roth Edmonds about the rival still reminds Lucas of the threat that this man's birth posed to his own marriage and family. After Roth was born and his mother died in the process, the baby, Lucas's wife Molly, and Lucas's son moved into the Edmonds house. Lucas became convinced that Molly and Zack Edmonds were lovers, and he risked his life to demand his family back and so challenge the white man's right to keep her. The nearly mortal struggle between Lucas and Zack ends with Lucas the victor, but he seems to know how hollow such a victory is in a system that grants and denies "manhood" based on racial identity:

> He breathed slow and quiet. *Women,* he thought. *Women. I wont never know. I dont want to. I ruther never to know than to find out later I have been fooled.* He turned toward the room where the fire was, where his supper waited. This time he spoke aloud. "How to God," he said, "can a black man ask a white man to please not lay down with his black wife? And even if he could ask it, how to God can the white man promise he wont?" (58)

"Pantaloon in Black" contains a similarly desperate misunderstanding between the races and a parallel misunderstanding between a man and his wife. The black mill worker Rider begins "Pantaloon" by burying his beloved wife of six months, and he ends it seared into the memory of a white deputy sheriff who sees him captured by a lynch mob and then tries to tell his unsympathetic wife about it. No one who sees Rider on this last day of his life understands that he grieves to remain living when Mannie is not, with her very footsteps "vanished but not gone" and "his body bursting the air her body had vacated, his eyes touching the objects – post and tree and field and house and hill – her eyes had lost" (133). He works to forget, he drinks to forget, he gambles to forget: nothing works until he commits a kind of suicide by killing the cheating white man who runs the dice game. To the deputy, black people "aint human" (149). "When it comes to the normal human feelings and sentiments of human beings, they might just as well be a damn herd of wild buffaloes," he says (149–50). To him, those normal feelings include taking a day off work to bury your wife, so his comments immediately discredit his point of view. But his extreme emotional response to Rider and the detail in which he describes what he has seen suggest that he has been more affected by what he has seen than perhaps he would like to admit. He keeps telling his story to a woman who keeps leaving the room and offers him nothing but disinterested and sarcastic disrespect when she enters it again. He may not understand what he sees of the end of Rider's life, but Faulkner means for us to feel Rider's misunderstood grief fully:

> "at last they had him down and Ketcham went in and there under the
> pile of them, laughing, with tears big as glass marbles running across his
> face and down past his ears and making a kind of popping sound on the
> floor like somebody dropping bird eggs, laughing and laughing and
> saying, 'Hit look lack Ah just cant quit thinking. Look lack Ah just cant
> quit.'"   (154)

The first three chapters of *Go Down, Moses* very carefully trace patterns of courtship and marriage, failed and successful, and patterns of racial behavior and their relationship to individual identity. The fourth chapter at last brings Isaac McCaslin directly into the action and makes the implicit motif of hunting in the first three even clearer. Buck chased Tomey's Turl; Turl chased Tennie; Sophonsiba chased Buck; Lucas chased treasure; Rider chased death. "The Old People" begins as Isaac kills his first buck and his mentor Sam Fathers marks him with its blood, making this an initiation story as obvious as the first three are subtle. The title connects Isaac to the other "old people" invoked earlier – Lucas, for example, and Carothers McCaslin, their mutual grandfather. It also brings the wilderness into the novel as a character on a par with the humans:

> There was only the soaring and somber solitude in the dim light, there
> was the thin murmur of the faint cold rain which had not ceased all day.
> Then, as if it had waited for them to find their positions and become
> still, the wilderness breathed again. It seemed to lean inward above
> them, above himself and Sam and Walter and Boon in their separate
> lurking-places, tremendous, attentive, impartial and omniscient; the
> buck moving in it somewhere, not running yet since he had not been
> pursued, not frightened yet and never fearsome but just alert as they
> were alert, perhaps already circling back, perhaps quite near, perhaps

conscious also of the eye of the ancient immortal Umpire . . . If there had been any sun, it would be near to setting now; there was a condensing, a densifying, of what he had thought was the gray and unchanging light until he realised suddenly that it was his own breathing, his heart, his blood – something, all things, and that Sam Fathers had marked him indeed, not as a mere hunter, but with something Sam had in his turn of his vanished and forgotten people. He stopped breathing then; there was only his heart, his blood, and in the following silence the wilderness ceased to breathe also, leaning, stopping overhead with its breath held, tremendous and impartial and waiting.   (174–5)

From Sam, Isaac has the wilderness as both teacher and legacy. From Cass, "rather his brother than cousin and rather his father than either" (4), he has the humanist tradition. He will spend his life in the midst of conflict between the two.

Cass and Isaac have their first philosophical discussion after the blood initiation and after Sam shows Isaac the magnificent buck that no one else sees. Isaac does not think that Cass believes in the buck, but Cass says, "Why not?":

> "Think of all that has happened here, on this earth . . . because after all you dont have to continue to bear what you believe is suffering; you can always choose to stop that, put an end to that. And even suffering and grieving is better than nothing; there is only one thing worse than not being alive, and that's shame. But you cant be alive forever, and you always wear out life long before you have exhausted the possibilities of living. And all that must be somewhere; all that could not have been invented and created just to be thrown away."   (178)

Besides, he says, "So did I. Sam took me in there once after I killed my first deer" (180). Cass will therefore listen to Isaac, offer him alternative interpretations of what he says, and respect his experience. This readiness to talk reflectively marks Cass's treatment of Isaac in the key scene in "The Bear" in which Isaac renounces his inheritance on his twenty-first birthday and refuses to accept ownership of the plantation. That scene begins the fourth section of "The Bear," the most famous and most complex section of the most famous and most complex chapter in the novel. The other sections frame the fourth section with the story of how Sam Fathers trained the great dog Lion to bring down Old Ben, "the big old bear with one trap-ruined foot that in an area almost a hundred miles square had earned for himself a name, a definite designation like a living man" (185). Old Ben, Lion, and Sam leave this world together, with only Isaac remaining as the designated heir to the wilderness that held them. Isaac accepts that legacy but rejects that of his grandfather because, he says, God meant man "to hold the earth mutual and intact in the communal anonymity of brotherhood" rather than pretend to own, sell, or bequeath it (246). He and Cass differ sharply on this matter, and behind both of their conflicting positions lies their awareness of "the ledgers in their scarred cracked leather bindings" and the story they contain of "the injustice and a little at least of its amelioration and restitution" (250). The ledgers record all of the business done on the plantation and its commissary. "The injustice" at first seems to refer to slavery, but as Isaac grows up reading and rereading the ledgers, he discovers "not only the general and condoned injustice and its slow amortization but the specific tragedy which had not been condoned and could never be amortized" (254). Isaac is used to the various injustices committed by his grandfather, including the bequest he left Tomey's Turl in his will: "*So I reckon that was cheaper than saying My son to a nigger* he thought. *Even if My son wasn't but just two words*" (258). But suddenly one day, while trying to imagine why his grandfather would have traveled all the way to New Orleans to buy a wife for a slave, Isaac leaps to "the specific tragedy" behind the records in the ledgers: "*His own daughter His own daughter. No No Not even him,*" he thinks, but "he knew from his own observation and memory that there had already been some white in Tomey's Terrel's blood before his father gave him the rest of it" (259). He concludes that Old Carothers committed not only miscegenation but incest.

The fourth section ends with the story of how Isaac McCaslin became "uncle to half a county and father to no one." He married a woman who wanted the McCaslin plantation, and when he would not get it back for her, she froze him out sexually: "'And that's all. That's all from me. If this dont get you that son you talk about, it wont be mine,' lying on her side, her back to the empty rented room, laughing and laughing" (301). Uncle to half the black and white population, as we discover in the ledgers, he loses the son he wanted in his turn. He claims to want peace, freedom, and brotherhood; in reality, he only sidesteps responsibility and shuffles it on to his cousin. Ironically, "the woods would be his mistress and his wife," in which he salutes a snake "evocative of all knowledge and an old weariness and of pariah-hood and death" exactly as Sam Fathers had saluted the mystical buck: "Chief," "Grandfather" (314).

The next chapter in the novel makes Isaac's ethical failure and overweening self-delusion even clearer. "Delta Autumn" follows him and his companions on a hunting trip to the Delta, the closest wilderness left. His great love for the wilderness remains, but it has subsumed every other memory or consideration in his life. He does not even care that mankind is destroying it "because there was just exactly enough of it" to last for his own lifetime. After that, he believes that he will enter "a dimension free of both time and space" with room for him and his "outlived" friends to "mov[e] again among the shades of tall unaxed trees and sightless brakes where the wild strong immortal game ran forever before the tireless belling immortal hounds, falling and rising phoenix-like to the soundless guns" (337–8). Isaac's vision of the eternal nonviolent hunt ignores the reality of the world in which he and others must live, and this becomes painfully clear when he meets the young lover of his kinsman, Roth. She holds their son in her arms. Roth has left her money and a one-word message: "No" (339). And even though Isaac has said that he believes that two people in love united sexually – "at the instant when it dont even matter whether they marry or not," as he puts it – "at that instant the two of them together were God," his true beliefs appear when the young woman mentions that her aunt took in washing: "He cried, not loud, in a voice of amazement, pity, and outrage: 'You're a nigger!'" (332, 344). In response, she tells him that James Beauchamp was her grandfather, that Roth does not know of their kinship, and that she and her child are going back north. When Isaac presses the money on her and tells her to marry "a man in your own race," her reply gives the lie to everything Isaac claims to believe about brotherhood: "Old man," she says, "have you lived so long and forgotten so much that you dont remember anything you ever knew or felt or even heard about love?" (346). The chapter closes with Isaac's fear of race-mixing, the news that Roth has just killed a doe, and Isaac himself back inside the cocoon of his bunk, hands crossed on his breast – a perfect image of his full retreat from life.

"Go Down, Moses" is the title of an African American spiritual that speaks to the slaves' yearning for freedom. The chorus is "Go down, Moses/Way down in Egypt land/Tell Old Pharaoh/To let my people go." At two key points in "The Old People," Faulkner alludes to that verse in his characterization of Sam Fathers as somehow caged or imprisoned by both his biracial heritage and the McCaslin family. Although Cass says, "His cage aint us" (162), Faulkner shows us that it is. Sam has to ask Cass for permission to move off the property to the hunting camp, for instance: "Let me go," he says (167). The final chapter of the novel also takes its name from the spiritual, and when Mollie Worsham asks lawyer Gavin Stevens to find her youngest grandchild, she says, "Roth Edmonds sold my Benjamin. Sold him in Egypt. Pharaoh got him" (354). She likens her troublemaking grandson to the younger son of Rachel and Jacob and sees Roth as a blood traitor. When Stevens discovers Butch's imminent execution in Chicago, he sets in motion an elaborate scheme to bring the body home yet keep the circumstances of the death from Mollie. The well-meaning Stevens thinks that he is acting honorably, but in reality he simply indulges a paternalistic racism: "They were like that," he generalizes (354) as he solicits funds "to bring a dead nigger home" (360). This categorical thinking keeps him not only from understanding Mollie's wishes but also from understanding her essential humanity. As her keening for Butch begins, Stevens defends "Mr Edmonds," but the song of mourning builds anyway, and it terrifies him so that he must run from the room (362–3). When the editor of the local newspaper tells him that Mollie wants him to print the whole story, Stevens can only retreat to more generalizations: "*she wanted him to come home right. She wanted that casket and those flowers and the hearse and she wanted to ride through town behind it in a car*" (365). Yet nowhere do we see Mollie ask for those things; Stevens wanted and got them, and for his own reasons, though even he might not know how to explain them. Like the ledgers at the heart of "The Bear," this novel is "that chronicle which was a whole land in miniature, which multiplied and compounded was the entire South" (280). And more than that: beginning as it does with the story of a conception and moving through marriages and liaisons across the color line and ending with a black woman's insistence that the public record contain the story of her grandson, *Go Down, Moses* identifies, pursues, and finally captures America's painful racial history.

Intruder in the Dust (1948)

Lucas Beauchamp returns to Faulkner's fiction in this novel to stand squarely at the center of its action yet unable to do very much in its pages: "It was just noon that Sunday morning when the sheriff reached the jail with Lucas Beauchamp though the whole town (the whole county too for that matter) had known since the night before that Lucas had killed a white man."[18] The first sentence of the novel highlights the idea of communal knowledge and then the rest of the novel dismantles it, for Lucas has not killed anyone. He knows who did, though, and to prove his innocence he draws on a debt of honor owed him by a young white boy, Chick Mallison, Gavin Stevens's nephew. Four years earlier, Chick fell into a creek near Lucas's house and then attempted to pay Lucas for his hospitality in drying him out and feeding him. Humiliated by Lucas's refusal to take the money and so admit his inferior racial status, Chick has never been able to assert any power over Lucas – as indeed no one has: "within the next year he was to learn every white man in that whole section of the country had been thinking about him for years: *We got to make him a nigger first. He's got to admit he's a nigger. Then maybe we will accept him as he seems to intend to be accepted*" (18). Chick wants this admission as well, but Lucas never makes it. He describes himself only as "a McCaslin" (19), and he sends Chick out to dig up the murdered man's grave to prove that "he wasn't shot with no fawty-one Colt" (68). How Chick would know, he does not say, but Chick does know the stakes for which he and Lucas now play: "the death by shameful violence of a man who would die not because he was a murderer but because his skin was black" (70–1).

Chick acquires two unlikely helpers, his black friend Aleck Sander and an old white woman named Miss Habersham, who help him to dig up the grave only to discover not the murdered man but another dead man. With this information they enlist the help of Stevens and the local sheriff, and when they all visit the grave again they encounter the murdered man's family. The town expects the Gowries to lynch Lucas for killing Vinson – they have even been joking about it – and the Gowries deeply resent the black convict labor the sheriff has brought to open their son's and brother's grave. Mr Gowrie has his twin sons do this, and they open the coffin lid on an empty box. They quickly find the first body and almost as quickly deduce that Vinson's must be in a nearby patch of quicksand. The detective work finishes rather quickly; they all know the name of the only person in the county who owned the type and caliber weapon that killed Vinson.

What remains for Faulkner to resolve is Chick's feelings about Lucas, his insistence that Lucas "be a nigger first." Chasing sleepless and frightened around the country on his behalf with a black boy and a woman who believes in Lucas's innocence changes Chick's perspective to such a degree that he can argue successfully with his garrulous uncle's racial views. Gavin would have the North leave the South alone to set "Sambo's" problems to rights (199). Chick sees matters in terms of simple justice and moral cowardice. He says that the crowds who would first lynch Lucas and then simply disappear when he is vindicated "were running from themselves. They ran home to hide their heads under the bedclothes from their own shame" (198). His next direct exchange with Lucas, the following Saturday in his uncle's office, demonstrates that Chick has decided to take Lucas on Lucas's terms:

> "Gentle-men," and then to him: "Young man – " courteous and intrac-
> table, more than bland: downright cheerful almost, removing the raked
> swagger of the hat: "You aint fell in no more creeks lately, have you?"
> "That's right," he said. "I'm saving that until you get some more ice on
> yours."
> "You'll be welcome without waiting for a freeze," Lucas said.   (235)

So does Lucas acknowledge Chick's manhood, in return for Chick acknowledg-ing his own. By contrast, lawyer Stevens tries to boss Lucas, telling him to take Miss Habersham some flowers and making him count out the money that Lucas insists on paying him for taking the case. Faulkner does not let Stevens domi-nate the scene, however; he disjoints the chronology of the story to embed its real-time ending in the middle of the story of Lucas's payment. Gavin patron-izes Lucas; he makes him count out every penny of the two dollars, for instance, saying "This is business" and then asking him, when he has finished, "What are you waiting for now?" Just as he did when confronted by another, more obvi-ous racist who called him a "goddamn biggity stiffnecked stinking burrheaded Edmonds sonofabitch" (19), Lucas has the last word, and the novel ends: "'My receipt,' Lucas said" (240–1).

Requiem for a Nun (1951)

Often described as a sequel to *Sanctuary*, Faulkner's fifteenth novel has a very unusual form. It is divided into three "acts," each beginning with a long prose section describing the history of Jefferson or Mississippi. The dramatic scenes following trace a time of crisis for the Stevens family, which includes lawyer Gavin, his nephew Gowan, and Gowan's wife Temple. The play opens as Nancy Mannigoe, former nanny and housekeeper to Gowan and Temple, is sentenced to death for murdering the Stevenses's infant daughter. A conflict between Gavin, who has defended Nancy in the case, and Temple ensues in which Gavin says that "Temple Drake" rather than "Mrs Gowan Stevens" should plead with the Governor to save Nancy's life.[19] When Gavin says that even such a strategy might not work, Temple quite reasonably asks him why she should try. He replies, "Truth," and "in quiet amazement," she responds:

> For no more than that. For no better reason than that. Just to get it told, breathed aloud, into words, sound. Just to be heard by, told to, someone, anyone, any stranger none of whose business it is, can possibly be, simply because he is capable of hearing, comprehending it. Why blink at your own rhetoric? Why dont you go on and tell me it's for the good of my soul – if I have one? (533)

By the end of the scene, we understand that something happened that Temple wants either to forget or to keep hidden, and Gavin thinks that that something is relevant to the murder of her child. We also see tension in the Stevens marriage.

As the dramatic scenes of the narrative unfold, Temple confesses to the Governor that at the age of seventeen she had an affair and wrote erotic letters to her lover. Recently, his brother discovered them and blackmailed her; they began an affair and planned to run away together, and to stop them Nancy killed the six-month-old girl. During her speeches, Gavin often interrupts her, either to add information or to prompt Temple. By the time she finishes, Gowan has replaced the Governor and heard the confession she had hoped to keep from him. Yet far from helping her or saving her soul, all the talking has done little more than depress Temple and raise even further doubts about the value of such a confession. At the end of Act II, for example, behaving "like a sleepwalker," she mumbles, "To save my soul – if I have a soul. If there is a God to save it – a God who wants it" (615). In Act III she asks Nancy:

> But why must it be suffering? He's omnipotent, or so they tell us. Why couldn't He have invented something else? Or, if it's got to be suffering, why cant it be just your own? Why cant you buy back your own sins with your own agony? Why do you and my little baby both have to suffer just because I decided to go to a baseball game eight years ago? Do you have to suffer everybody else's anguish just to believe in God? What kind of God is it that has to blackmail His customers with the whole world's grief and ruin?   (658)

Nancy's simple answer, "Believe" (663), does not answer Temple's questions. Indeed, they have no answer in the novel. Temple echoes Macbeth in her state of existential terror: "there's still tomorrow and tomorrow. And suppose tomorrow and tomorrow, and then nobody there, nobody waiting to forgive me" (662). Temple can only join her husband and his uncle, and the novel ends as the sound of their footsteps fades away.

The prose sections of the novel contain implicit responses to Temple's doubts, for they record the stories of individuals who have marked history in some way. If you cannot be certain of God, you can recover as best you can the stories of men and women like you. Such recovery and restoration of narrative seem to be the real point of the elaborate prologues to each act, each of which focuses on a building that serves as a kind of set for the ensuing dialogue. Act I, "The Courthouse," recounts how Jefferson got its name and therefore its beginnings as an idea in the minds of the men who built it:

> – not even speaking for a while yet since each one probably believed (a little shamefaced too) that the thought was solitarily his, until at last one spoke for all and then it was all right since it had taken one conjoined breath to shape that sound, as you insert the first light tentative push of wind into the mouthpiece of a strange untried foxhorn: "By God. Jefferson."
>
> "Jefferson, Mississippi," a second added.
>
> "Jefferson, Yoknapatawpha County, Mississippi," a third corrected; who, which one, didn't matter this time either since it was still one conjoined breathing . . .   (495)

Act II, "The Golden Dome," describes the state capitol building as "the gilded pustule . . . incapable of being either looked full or evaded" that presides over a state whose "diversions" are religion and politics; Temple's confession takes place there. Finally, Act III, "The Jail," emerges as the place that has "seen all: the mutation and the change: and, in that sense, had recorded them" (616). That building "records" Temple's last conversation with Nancy. If she had known to go into the jailer's residence and look, Temple could have found one response to the possibility of oblivion, and that is to make a gesture that speaks to someone else's imagination, as Cecilia Farmer did in 1861 when she scratched her name in a windowpane:

> a fragile workless scratching almost depthless in a sheet of old barely transparent glass, and (all you had to do was look at it a while; all you have to do now is remember it) there is the clear undistanced voice as though out of the delicate antenna-skeins of radio, further than empress's throne, than splendid satiation, even than matriarch's peaceful rocking chair, across the vast instantaneous intervention, from the long long time ago: *"Listen, stranger; this was myself: this was I."*   (649)

Across time and geographical distance, a stranger to Jefferson hears Cecilia's voice, feels her very essence, and will call the experience to mind when he needs it. The memory, the "one conjoined breathing," lives on.

A Fable (1954)

Without doubt, Faulkner's sixteenth novel took him the longest to produce, caused him the most worry and self-doubt, and – despite the fact that it won the Pultizer Prize and the National Book Award – for all that effort impressed the reading public the least of any book in his career. Foremost is the problem of how to describe it to someone else. Like *Absalom, Absalom!* and *The Unvanquished*, it is a novel about a war central to a culture's demolition. Like *The Sound and the Fury* and *Go Down, Moses*, it is a novel about generational conflict. Like *Flags in the Dust/Sartoris*, it concerns survivors of the Great War; it also contains an embedded story about a stolen racehorse that anticipates *The Reivers*. Yet *A Fable* also contains at its heart an allegory of the Christ story in which a corporal leads a platoon of twelve men in an effort to convince both sides not to fight any more – an effort which accomplishes nothing but the assassination of his commanding general, his own execution for mutiny, and the destruction of unarmed men who try to follow him into noncombat. This plot absorbed Faulkner from 1943, when he and two filmmakers got the idea for a script about France's Unknown Soldier, until the publication of *A Fable* in 1954. It absorbed him to such an extent that he outlined it in pencil on the walls of his office at Rowan Oak. He literally lived out his days under the skeleton of this book.

Yet looked at as a skeleton, some real sense begins to emerge from the welter of plot details and unnamed characters that comprise this novel. The book begins on "Wednesday," the day the mutinying regiment is taken to the battlefield capital of Chaulnesmont, and then backtracks to "Monday/Monday Night," when the regiment mutinied. Faulkner then switches to a new set of characters, two British privates on "Tuesday Night." He continues to move between parts of days in this fateful Easter week: Thursday, when the troops refuse to fight, and in the evening General Gragnon is assassinated; Friday, when the corporal is executed alongside criminals; Saturday, when three women take him for burial; and the final chapter "Tomorrow," in which a detail of twelve drunken soldiers charged with finding an anonymous French soldier's corpse for the Tomb instead produces an Eastern European corporal, who has been blown out of his grave by the resumed hostilities. The naming of chapters after days and sections of days suggests that Faulkner was less interested in representing chronology than in seeing what disjointing and reassembling it in certain patterns would allow him to accomplish. He was making a novel about time out of units of time, much as his earlier episodic fiction had made novels about important moments out of important moments.

The novel has provoked discussion for the fifty-plus years of its published life, and increasingly critics read it as Faulkner's examination of various kinds of group-speak – as the indictment of war he claimed, and as an indictment of the mindless power of obedient crowds, so easily manipulated by those who wield a culture's ideological weapons. If it takes time for individuals in this novel to come to a reader's attention in such masses of people, so, too, does it take time for an individual to respond to and decide to do something about a chaotic situation in life. Modern people, like Eliot's Prufrock, often melt into groups even as they wish they could stand out from them, and they do this for many reasons – safety, fear, even love and compassion. These traits mark all of the troops in the war, as seen in the passage describing their attempt to stop it:

> not his haste but one haste, not only the battalion but the German one or regiment or whatever it was, the two of them running toward each other now, empty-handed, approaching until he could see, distinguish the individual faces but still all one face, one expression, and then he knew suddenly that his too looked like that, all of them did: tentative, amazed, defenseless, and then he heard the voices too and knew that his was one also – a thin murmuring sound rising into the incredible silence like a chirping of lost birds, forlorn and defenseless too . . .[20]

In the next second "the frantic uprush of the rockets from behind the two wires, German and British too" kills all of them. Acting as a snare for people of all ideological types, time in this novel is cyclical: the "tomorrow" that so bores Macbeth and worries Temple Drake Stevens in *Requiem for a Nun* stretches endlessly ahead, unredeemed by the corporal or anyone else.

The Town (1957)

The Town is dedicated to Faulkner's lifelong friend and early mentor, Phil Stone, who "did half the laughing for thirty years."[21] That dedication acknowledges the funny Snopes stories that Faulkner wrote over the course of his entire career, many of which undergird all three of the novels in the so-called "Snopes Trilogy." *The Town* opens with a revised version of "Centaur in Brass," a story first published in *American Mercury* magazine in 1932. That story describes how Flem Snopes's plan to steal brass from the Jefferson power plant is foiled by the very two men he manipulated in order to carry it out. As the opening of this novel, however, Faulkner revised a great deal of the humor out of it in order to reflect his more serious concerns with Flem's gradual rise to power in Jefferson. The episodes in this book have three narrators, attorney Gavin Stevens, Gavin's nephew Chick Mallison, and sewing-machine agent V. K. Ratliff. They trade information about Flem and his relatives, and early on we get an indication that Gavin, for one, has stopped finding them funny. "You used to laugh at them too," Ratliff says, and Gavin replies, a little desperately, "What else are we going to do about them? Of course you've got the best joke: you dont have to fry hamburgers anymore. But give them time; maybe they have got one taking a correspondence school law course. Then I wont have to be acting city attorney anymore either" (39). Ratliff, who got a powerful comeuppance at Flem's hands in *The Hamlet*, has now distanced himself completely from the Snopeses. He can keep laughing, or at least watch what they do with some clarity of perspective. Gavin, however, has fallen in love with Eula Varner Snopes, who in turn has had an eighteen-year love affair with Manfred de Spain. Where the Eula of *The Hamlet* was so passive that she refused to walk as a child, this Eula acts how she chooses, up to a point. She dances with De Spain in public "because she was alive and not ashamed of it" (66), and even young Chick can imagine a grown man, even her lover, saying, "Hold on here; have I maybe blundered into something not just purer than me but even braver than me, braver and tougher than me because it is purer than me, cleaner than me? Because that's what it was" that makes her unforgettable (65).

Indeed, as Gavin and Ratliff and Chick learn more about Flem's emotional chokehold on Eula's daughter, the stories of *The Town* lead up to and then away from Eula's grave. As Faulkner telegraphed his publisher in August 1956: "FINISH BOOK TODAY. WILL BREAK THE HEART. THOUGHT IT WAS JUST FUNNY BUT WAS WRONG" (*SL* 403). This novel grieves a lost love as surely as does *Absalom, Absalom!*, as Gavin mourns Eula's death as his own failing:

> I watched her, through the gate and up the walk, losing dimension now, onto or rather into the shadow of the little gallery and losing even substance now. And then I heard the door and it was as if she had not been . . . a dimension less, then a substance less, then the sound of a door and then, not *never been* but simply *no more is* since always and forever that *was* remains, as if what is going to happen to one tomorrow already gleams faintly visible now if the watcher were only wise enough to discern it or maybe just brave enough. (293)

The novel ends with Gavin unable to understand anything about Eula's life or death, and with Jefferson's experience with "four Snopes Indians or Indian Snopeses, whichever is right" – Byron Snopes's murderous children sent to Flem, who characteristically refuses to accept responsibility for those relatives who, like the murdering Mink, can be of no advantage to him (319). Ratliff makes Chick and Gavin an offer: "Would either of you gentlemen like to go down with me and watch what they call the end of a erea, if that's what they call what I'm trying to say? The last and final end of Snopes out-and-out unvarnished behavior in Jefferson, if that's what I'm trying to say?" (325). As Ratliff knows, Flem has won again, if not as decisively as he did in *The Hamlet,* and watching him from now on will be a coalition that understands the measures he is willing to take as he moves toward what Ratliff might call a "varnished," or publicly respectable, life as the president of a Jefferson bank.

The Mansion (1959)

Divided into three named books and narrated primarily by V. K. Ratliff, Gavin Stevens, Chick Mallison, and a third-person narrator, *The Mansion* begins with Faulkner's prefatory note admitting the "discrepancies and contradictions in the thirty-four year progress of this particular chronicle" of *Snopes.*[22] He called the novel "the final chapter of, and the summation of, a work conceived and begun in 1925" and accounted for changes in the story as inevitable in an "entire life's work" in "a living literature." Besides, he wrote,

> the author has already found more discrepancies and contradictions
> than he hopes the reader will – contradictions and discrepancies due
> to the fact that the author has learned, he believes, more about the
> human heart and its dilemma than he knew thirty-four years ago; and is
> sure that, having lived with them that long time, he knows the characters
> in this chronicle better than he did then.   (331)

Readers who notice, for example, that in *The Hamlet* Mink Snopes kills Jack
Houston but in *The Mansion* kills Zack Houston should therefore either forget the detail or just get over the discrepancy. Faulkner has other and more
important matters on his mind.

"Mink," the first book of the novel, traces Mink's life from the time he kills
Houston until he gets out of Parchman Penitentiary thirty-eight years later.
Mink trusted in his cousin Flem to keep him out of jail in the first place, and
when he realizes that Flem has no intention of helping him, Mink forms a plan:
"*It looks like I done had to come all the way to Parchman jest to turn right around
and go back home and kill Flem*" (377). Flem seems to divine Mink's plan,
because he arranges an elaborate escape plot involving another Snopes "uncle
or cousin" (389) – no outsider really understands the Snopes genealogy – also
on the wrong side of the law. Montgomery Ward Snopes has been operating a
peep show of obscene French postcards in Jefferson, and Flem blackmails him
into a prison term at Parchman so that he can set Mink up for an additional
twenty-year sentence. In a surprising and unprecedented chapter, the escape
plot is narrated by none other than Montgomery Ward Snopes. It is the only
time in Faulkner's career that he lets a Snopes narrate, and the decision results
in some of his best comic fiction. Montgomery Ward summarizes the essence
of what makes a Snopes a Snopes: "every Snopes has one thing he wont do to
you – provided you can find out what it is before he has ruined and wrecked
you" (392), for example, and

> I dont remember when it was, I was probably pretty young, when I
> realised that I had come from what you might call a family, a clan, a race,
> maybe even a species, of pure sons of bitches. So I said, *Okay, okay, if
> that's the way it is, we'll just show them. They call the best of lawyers,
> lawyers' lawyers and the best of actors an actor's actor and the best of
> athletes a ball-player's ball-player. All right, that's what we'll do: every
> Snopes will make it his private and personal aim to have the whole world
> recognise him as THE son of a bitch's son of a bitch.*   (409–10)

Seeing the Snopes family from the inside out, filtered through the point of
view of this cynically self-aware and intelligent man, readers find more fully
developed and humanized characters and fewer comic ciphers. Similarly, the
evolving portrait of Mink gradually reveals a single-minded but emotionally

complex man. When he gets out of jail in October, for example, he realizes that he has forgotten the existence of seasons. As a free man, "now they belonged to him again"; "back home in the hills, all the land would be gold and crimson with hickory and gum and oak and maple, and the old fields warm with sage and splattered with scarlet sumac; in thirty-eight years he had forgotten that" (425–6). In the midst of other things he has forgotten, Mink remembers his stepmother, "lachrymose, harassed, yet constant," for whom he had once killed a squirrel to eat because his father had beaten her too hard for her to eat their regular coarse food. He thinks of the tree in which he found the squirrel, realizing consciously that it has probably been cut down but suddenly understanding that it still stands "unaxed in memory and unaxeable, inviolable and immune, golden and splendid with October": "*Why yes* he thought; *it aint a place a man wants to go back to; the place dont even need to be there no more. What aches a man to go back to is what he remembers*" (427). Capable of such moving insight, Mink nonetheless stays his course to kill Flem, and his book ends with him on the way to Memphis to buy a gun.

"Linda" tells the story of Flem's daughter's return to Jefferson after her wounding on the front during the Spanish Civil War. Everyone in town knows that Flem is not Linda's biological father, but no one in town knows how Linda feels about this. Readers of "Mink" know that "Linda Snopes Kohl" has generated a petition for Mink's early release, and her section ends on the ominous suggestion that Linda has plans that will upset Jefferson generally and Gavin in particular: "She aint going to marry him," Ratliff tells Chick, "It's going to be worse than that" (562). "Flem" begins by returning to Mink's inexorable journey toward Jefferson and then moves to the response of citizens there to the news that he has been released – most specifically, to Gavin's. He warns Flem; he tells the local sheriff to set up roadblocks; he tries to hide the news from Linda. Yet none of Gavin's actions deters either Mink or Linda, who has planned her "father's" murder just as carefully as Mink has. Her revenge accomplished, she leaves Jefferson for good, and Ratliff and Gavin bring payoff money to Mink. The novel closes with this dangerous yet oddly compelling little man walking west because "*I'm free now. I can walk any way I want to*" (720) and then, when he wants to, lying down to arrange himself for sleep:

> it seemed to him he could feel the Mink Snopes that had had to spend so much of his life just having unnecessary bother and trouble, beginning to creep, seep, flow easy as sleeping; he could almost watch it, following all the little grass blades and tiny roots, the little holes the worms made, down and down into the ground already full of the folks that had the trouble but were free now, so that it was just the ground and the dirt that had to bother and worry and anguish with the passions and hopes and

> skeers, the justice and the injustice and the griefs, leaving the folks
> themselves easy now, all mixed and jumbled up comfortable and easy
> so wouldn't nobody even know or even care who was which anymore,
> himself among them, equal to any, good as any, brave as any, being
> inextricable from, anonymous with all of them: the beautiful, the
> splendid, the proud and the brave, right on up to the very top itself
> among the shining phantoms and dreams which are the milestones of
> the long human recording – Helen and the bishops, the kings and the
> unhomed angels, the scornful and graceless seraphim.   (720–1)

In this lyrical passage Faulkner's one-of-a-kind Mink Snopes joins the speaker of Walt Whitman's *Song of Myself* in the common, binding, and ultimately deathless metaphor of the grass. In the process Faulkner evokes Mark Twain's Huck Finn, whose vernacular narration revolutionized American literature and who like Mink prefers things "mixed and jumbled up comfortable and easy." The mention of Helen, to whom Eula is so often compared in this novel, links Mink's story with the Homeric and then the biblical legends that represent the best of the stories that men and women have told one another about each other. In his penultimate novel, then, Faulkner writes his Snopeses into the "long recording" that precedes and will forever after contain them.

The Reivers (1962)

In a 1955 interview Faulkner said, "My last book will be the Doomsday book, the Golden Book, of Yoknapatawpha County. Then I shall break the pencil and I'll have to stop" (*LIG* 255). For years *The Reivers* has been read just that way, in spite of the fact that Faulkner lived for another seven years after the comment, publishing two more novels in the process, and in spite of the fact that a scholar demonstrated fairly early on that Faulkner had no real plans for such a volume. *The Reivers* does contain recastings and retellings of many familiar Yoknapatawpha moments, including stories of Hightowers, Compsons, and McCaslins, but Faulkner did not intend it to be his last novel. He simply passed away before he wrote another one.

"Grandfather said:": the first line of the novel, with its introductory colon, sets up an elaborate frame tale in which characters emerge as composites of the stories that others know about them.[23] Boon Hogganbeck, "a corporation" maintained by three Jefferson families (737), serves as the first extended example of this. "This is the kind of man Boon Hogganbeck was. Hung on the wall, it could have been his epitaph" (725), and what follows is a funny story about Boon trying to avenge himself for a racial insult by attempting to shoot a fellow employee. A notoriously bad shot, Boon misses his intended target but hits an innocent bystander, and the episode has the whole town in an uproar:

> They were all there, black and white: one crowd where Mr Hampton . . . and two or three bystanders wrestling with Boon, and another crowd where another deputy was holding Ludus about twenty feet away and still in the frozen attitude of running or frozen in the attitude of running or in the attitude of frozen running, whichever is right, and another crowd around the window of Cousin Ike's store which one of Boon's bullets (they never did find where the other four went) had shattered after creasing the buttock of a Negro girl who was now lying on the pavement screaming until Cousin Ike himself came jumping out of the store and drowned her voice with his, roaring with rage at Boon not for ruining the window but (Cousin Ike was young then but already the best woodsman and hunter this county ever had) for being unable to hit with five shots an object only twenty feet away. (734)

Typical of Faulkner's tendency to describe scenes of frantic motion by freezing the action and describing it from several angles, this scene also contains Faulkner's playful parodying of his own technique – the variants of "frozen running, whichever is right." More seriously, the story introduces the themes of race and class inequity that will run throughout this novel. Boon, who has Indian and white ancestors, claims to be a white man when it suits him, as it does when Ludus insults him: "Me, a white man, have got to stand here and let a damn mule-wrestling nigger either criticise my private tail, or state before five public witnesses that I aint got any sense" (735). The black or mulatto characters in this novel do not have that luxury, as John Powell knows when he carries his pistol, "the living badge of his manhood" (728), to work every day even though he must hide it in deference to the "manhood" of his white employer. These rather obvious Freudian jokes disguise some hard truths about what it means to be a man in 1905 Jefferson. Lip service to the gentlemanly code of "*entendre-de-noblesse*" – what the nobility understands as its obligations to the lower classes – appears to transcend racial lines: at one point John refuses to say "Mister" when he refers to Boon, "something he would never have failed to do in the hearing of any white man he considered his equal, because John was a gentleman" (730). Near the end of the novel, our eleven-year-old protagonist gets some advice from his grandfather that seems to validate that code. Whatever your mistakes, Boss Priest says, you've got to "Live with it"; "A gentleman accepts the responsibility of his actions and bears the burden of their consequences, even when he did not himself instigate them but only acquiesced to them, didn't say No though he knew he should" (968–9). What happens during the course of the novel, between those two tributes to gentle-manliness, tests that system and finds it wanting.

And what happens during the course of this novel is a brilliantly plotted coming-of-age story in which young Lucius Priest, the narrating "Grandfather" of the first line, takes a road trip to Memphis in his grandfather's "borrowed" automobile with Boon Hogganbeck and the black family retainer Ned William McCaslin. When they get there they proceed directly to Miss Reba's whore-house, where Boon has a girl. Ned swaps the automobile for a stolen thor-oughbred racehorse, and in order to set things right, Lucius ends up riding that horse in several races. Of course, the schemes are discovered. The novel ends with Boon married to his girl, Everbe Corinthia, and the birth of their child "Lucius Priest Hogganbeck" (971). Ned even ends up making money on the races. Structurally a comedy, then, *The Reivers* finds Lucius learning some decidedly unfunny things about life as an adult. First, he learns how to lie like an adult – to get what he wants rather than to defend himself – and the trip he takes leads him to learn about the existence of whorehouses. When he meets the landlord of Miss Reba's, he hears a man talk to and about women in ways he has never heard before: "The trouble with you bitches is, you have to act like ladies some of the time but you dont know how"; "The trouble with you ladies is, you dont know how to quit acting like bitches." Lucius has a ready sympathy for the victim of this language: "nobody should ever have to be that alone, nobody, not ever" (813). His sympathy turns into outraged vengeance when a morally "wizened ten-year-old boy" tells him about "pugnuckling," the activity engaged in by Miss Corrie, with whom he has fallen in love (851). More to the point, when he hears about sexual voyeurism from this same boy, he tries to "destroy" the bearer of this news and "all who had participated in her debasement: not only the two panders, but the insensitive blackguard chil-dren and the brutal and shameless men who paid their pennies to watch her defenseless and undefended and unavenged degradation" (852). Then, swept into riding in the horse races, Lucius further learns that representatives of the "Law" will extort sex from women; that white "Law" similarly practices racial extortion against decent and dignified members of the community; that men whom he loves, like Boon and Ned, think that beating women "dont break nothing" (937); and that he himself, by virtue of simply being alive, belongs to that whole sorry company:

> But I was more than afraid. I was ashamed that such a reason for fearing
> for Uncle Parsham, who had to live here, existed; hating . . . it all, hating
> all of us for being the poor frail victims of being alive, having to be
> alive – hating Everbe for being the vulnerable helpless lodestar victim;

and Boon for being the vulnerable and helpless victimised; and Uncle Parsham and Lycurgus for being where they had to, couldn't help but, watch white people behaving exactly as white people bragged that only Negroes behaved – just as I had hated Otis for telling me about Everbe in Arkansas and hated Everbe for being that helpless lodestar for human debasement which he had told me about and hated myself for listening, having to hear about it, know about it; hating that such not only was, but must be, had to be if living was to continue and mankind be a part of it. (865–6)

"To reive" is an old Scottish verb meaning "to steal," "to take away by stealth." An accidental reiver at first, Lucius learns of his own complicity in human injustice, if not outright evil, the hardest lesson of all.

That lesson sits at the structural center of *The Reivers*, and in that moment Lucius's childhood ends. The rest of the novel traces what Lucius does with the almost unbearable pull toward misanthropy, and his action parallels the promise that Everbe makes him to give up prostitution: "You can choose," she says, "you can decide. You can say No. You can find a job and work" (854). Grown-ups can and must do this and sometimes even more, as Lucius discovers when he realizes that Ned has come to Memphis not just because he "wants a trip too" (781) but because he has a kinsman in trouble with a white man. Other white men keep his racehorse scheme from working, but Ned never quits, and Lucius finally realizes the enormity of his effort of "four days . . . during which Ned had carried the load alone, held back the flood, shored up the crumbling levee with whatever tools he could reach – including me – until they broke in his hand" (970). Like Everbe, Ned "can say No" to circumstances as he finds them. Lucius takes this as a final lesson from his trip to Memphis: "your outside is just what you live in, sleep in, and has little connection with who you are and even less with what you do" (970). By this he does not mean that a person's race, class, sex, or age does not affect their identity or their circumstances in life. He means, rather, that human change is internal, mental, emotional, invisible to the eye – but painfully real, for all of that.

Short stories

Faulkner wrote short fiction throughout his career, and today readers will probably encounter examples of it in several volumes of collections or in anthologies. During his lifetime, Faulkner oversaw the construction and publication of five volumes of his short stories (the largest of which is *Collected Stories* [1950]) and two collections that included some of them along with excerpts from longer fiction (*The Portable Faulkner* and *The Faulkner Reader* [1954]). Such excerpts have also been printed, misleadingly, as self-contained units of shorter fiction; for example, the Vintage paperback *Three Famous Short Novels* contains "Spotted Horses," "Old Man," and "The Bear," from *The Hamlet, If I Forget Thee, Jerusalem (The Wild Palms)*, and *Go Down, Moses*, respectively. Of those pieces conceived and published as short stories, "A Rose for Emily," "Barn Burning," "Turnabout," "Wash," "Two Soldiers," and "That Evening Sun" appear most often in anthologies as representative of Faulkner's fiction.

Faulkner's first short story to appear in a national magazine, "A Rose for Emily," has been reprinted and discussed more often than any of his other stories. It describes the changing fortunes of Emily Grierson, the only child of a domineering man: "We remembered all the young men her father had driven away," the narrator says, "and we knew that with nothing left, she would have to cling to that which had robbed her, as people will."[24] Emily goes from sought-after young woman to orphan to spinster, and during her transition to the latter phase she has a brief affair with a "Yankee" named Homer Barron (124), who disappears from Jefferson. The townspeople, represented in the text by the narrator, keep an eye on Emily:

> When we next saw Miss Emily, she had grown fat and her hair was turning gray. During the next few years it grew grayer and grayer until it attained an even pepper-and-salt iron-gray, when it ceased turning. Up to the day of her death at seventy-four it was still that vigorous iron-gray, like the hair of an active man.   (127–8)

So does the narrator plant the first clue to the truth of Homer Barron's disappearance immediately after mentioning it, apparently in passing, and the story closes with our narrator among a group in Miss Emily's bedroom after her funeral, gazing at a dead man in the bed with "a long strand of iron-gray hair" on the pillow beside him (130). The horror-movie quality of the scene makes "A Rose for Emily" somewhat unusual in Faulkner's career, but Faulkner's other successful fictions, short and long, also benefit from the perfect timing of the complex narration and the careful withholding of the truth of the life that Emily really lives behind the doors that Jefferson watches so closely. No matter how much we think we know about someone else, Faulkner seems to say, we really do not know how it feels to be someone else.

That kind of intense, quickly drawn, yet deeply felt empathy marks all of Faulkner's work. "Barn Burning," for example, introduces Colonel Sartoris Snopes, a ten-year-old boy torn between loyalty to his father and a more abstract sense of what constitutes justice in the world. When his father seeks justice, he burns barns; on one such occasion he hit Sarty when it seemed as though Sarty would have confirmed this in court. "You've got to learn to stick to your own blood or you ain't going to have any blood to stick to you," Abner tells him as the first lesson in "getting to be a man" (*CS* 8). Sarty feels nothing but hopeless in this situation:

> it was as if the blow and the following calm, outrageous voice still rang, repercussed, divulging nothing to him save the terrible handicap of being young, the light weight of his few years, just heavy enough to prevent his soaring free of the world as it seemed to be ordered but not heavy enough to keep him footed solid in it, to resist it and try to change the course of its events. (9)

In "Turnabout," set among pilots in the Great War, the American captain Bogard learns a similar kind of lesson in powerlessness when he hears of the deaths of two British torpedo boat pilots. He has been on a mission with them and seen firsthand the inferior tools with which the men have been asked to complete some of the most dangerous missions in the war, and when he hears of their deaths he leads a raid on a château of enemy generals: "Then his hand dropped and he zoomed, and he held the aeroplane so, in its wild snarl, his lips parted, his breath hissing, thinking, 'God! God! If they were all there – all the generals, the admirals, the presidents and the kings – theirs, ours – all of them'" (509). A capable and brave pilot, Bogard can no more stop the war than Sarty can stop Ab from burning Major de Spain's barn.

"Two Soldiers" shows the positive, character-building possibilities in family loyalty, as a young unnamed narrator describes how his brother Pete enlisted in the Army after the Japanese attack on Pearl Harbor in 1941. When Pete leaves, his mother tells him, "Don't never forget who you are. You ain't rich and the rest of the world outside Frenchman's Bend never heard of you. But your blood is good as any blood anywhere, and don't you ever forget it" (87). His father agrees: "Always remember what your ma told you and write her whenever you find the time" (87). But the nearly nine-year-old narrator goes so far as to follow Pete to Memphis, where he believes that he will join him "on the way to Pearl Harbor" (95) – hence the two soldiers of the title.

The setting of the story in Frenchman's Bend links it with Faulkner's Snopes novels, *As I Lay Dying*, and *Sanctuary*, as well as with other short fiction set in small poor rural areas such as "Shingles for the Lord" and "Wash." The latter story, with important connections to *Absalom, Absalom!*, describes the inner life of a man whom everyone in the story would characterize as "white trash" (536). He can bear the injustice of his life because of his identification with Colonel Thomas Sutpen:

> It would seem to him that that world in which Negroes, whom the Bible
> told him had been created and cursed by God to be brute and vassal to
> all men of white skin, were better found and housed and even clothed
> than he and his; that world in which he sensed always about him
> mocking echoes of black laughter was but a dream and an illusion,
> and that the actual world was this one across which his own lonely
> apotheosis seemed to gallop on the black thoroughbred.   (538)

When Sutpen impregnates and then abandons his granddaughter, Wash's illusions collapse, and he realizes that Sutpen oppresses him as surely as he does the slaves on the plantation: "*Better if his kind and mine too had never drawn the breath of life on this earth. Better that all who remain of us be blasted from the face of the earth than that another Wash Jones should see his whole life shredded from him and shrivel away like a dried shuck thrown onto the fire*" (549). In "That Evening Sun" the young narrator Quentin makes a parallel realization about racial realities in Jefferson. The black sometime-prostitute Nancy occasionally cooks for Quentin's family, and he hears a conversation once between her and her husband Jesus regarding her pregnancy. When Jesus says that he can "cut down the vine" that made her pregnant, he adds, "When white man want to come in my house, I aint got no house" (292), and the truth of that statement shocks Quentin so deeply that it even changes the syntax and style of his narration. The story that he tells of Nancy's terror of Jesus scares him so badly that he abandons the highly literate style of the first pages for plain, repetitive reportage and dialogue (289–92). A member of the race that subordinates and abandons Nancy, Quentin sees his place in the guilty design of his culture. The barber Hawkshaw makes a similar discovery in "Dry September," when he not only stops protesting the innocence of a black man accused of "something" with "Miss Minnie Cooper," a white spinster, and summarily lynched. When the man strikes out at his kidnappers, he hits Hawkshaw, "and the barber struck him also" (178). His action marks him as complicit; the realization sickens him.

Yet not all of Faulkner's short stories have such grim parameters. He wrote very good detective fiction, for example, in which local knowledge and expertise foil plots to get away with extortion and murder; such are the stories collected into *Knight's Gambit* (1949). He also created occasional humor running from the mock heroic, in stories such as "A Courtship," which details the rivalry between an Indian and a white man for the attentions of an Indian woman who marries someone else, to the scatological, such as "Afternoon of a Cow," in which a cow poops all over a man named Faulkner, and "My Grandmother Millard and General Bedford Forrest and the Battle of Harrykin Creek," in which a young soldier's last name of Backhouse nearly derails his courtship of a young lady found by the Yankees in one of the same. He used race to humorous effect, as in "Centaur in Brass," wherein two black co-workers foil Flem Snopes's plan to steal brass from the city power plant, and "Lo!," which describes how Indians outwit the President of the United States by pretending to be as simple-minded as he thinks they are. He showed the funny aspects of the wars between men and women in "Mule in the Yard" when Mrs Mannie Hait gets the better of mule trader I. O. Snopes. And in the process time and again Faulkner used the techniques found in his great tragic fiction for humorous ends, as in this passage from "Shingles for the Lord," in which he freezes the furious motion of a church catching on fire and tells it from the point of view of a young boy suspended over it with his father:

> when he lunged back he snatched that whole section of roof from around the lantern like you would shuck a corn nubbin. The lantern was hanging on a nail. He never even moved the nail, he jest pulled the board off it, so that it looked like for a whole minute I watched the lantern, and the crowbar, too, setting there in the empty air in a little mess of floating shingles, with the empty nail still sticking through the bail of the lantern, before the whole thing started down into the church. It hit the floor and bounced once. Then it hit the floor again, and this time the whole church jest blowed up into a pit of yellow jumping fire, with me and pap hanging over the edge of it on two ropes.
>
> I don't know what become of the rope nor how we got out of it. I don't remember climbing down. Jest pap yelling behind me and pushing me about halfway down the ladder and then throwing me the rest of the way by a handful of my overhalls, and then we was both on the ground, running for the water barrel . . . And I believe we still would have put it out. Pap turned and squatted against the barrel and got a holt of it over his shoulder and stood up with that barrel that was almost full and run around the corner and up the steps of the church and hooked his toe on the top step and come down with the barrel busting on top of him and knocking him out cold as a wedge.   (39)

Whereas Faulkner's ability to build a story toward a climactic, final one-liner can work to frighten readers of "A Rose for Emily" and to sound the anxious notes of the final lines of *Absalom, Absalom!* that force a rereading of what precedes them, the same ability can make us laugh. Of Mrs Hait's victory in "Mule in the Yard," Old Het says, "de mule burnt de house and you shot de mule. Dat's whut I calls justice" (264). And thoroughly exasperated at the end of a day that has seen him matching wits with a disgruntled former Works Progress Administration worker and burning down his own community's church, Pap says, "Arsonist," recalling what the minister has just called him, "Work units. Dog units. And now arsonist. I Godfrey, what a day!" (43).

Comic, tragic, wry, bitter, ironic, or just plain weird, Faulkner's short stories contain some of his most moving plots and compelling prose. The idea of collecting the short stories came from one of Faulkner's editors, but he embraced the project and even suggested a separate collection of Gavin Stevens detective stories (*Knight's Gambit*). His comments on the collecting process reveal his customary fascination with the organization of his material. He explained to Malcolm Cowley that "even to a collection of stories, form, integration, is as important as to a novel – an entity of its own, single, set for one pitch, contrapuntal in organization, toward one end, one finale" (*SL* 278). Those comments recall the explanations he gave for the unusual form of *If I Forget Thee, Jerusalem (The Wild Palms)*. The form of *Collected Stories* itself divides into named miniature worlds: "The Country," "The Village," "The Wilderness," "The Waste Land," "The Middle Ground," and "Beyond." "The Country" begins with "Barn Burning," sounding themes that other sections will modify, and "Beyond" ends with the poetical and mystical "Carcassonne," its protagonist contemplating his desire "*to perform something bold and tragical and austere*" (*CS* 899) – a desire that reflects an artistic nature in search of ways to express itself. When asked to explain the genesis of what an interviewer called "the Yoknapatawpha saga," Faulkner invoked the image of himself as the creator of a cosmos:

> Beginning with *Sartoris* I discovered that my own little postage stamp of native soil was worth writing about and that I would never live long enough to exhaust it, and by sublimating the actual to the apocryphal I would have complete liberty to use whatever talent I might have to its absolute top. It opened up a gold mine of other peoples, so I created a cosmos of my own. I can move those people around like God, not only in space but in time too . . . I like to think of the world I created as being a kind of keystone in the Universe; that, as small as that keystone is, if it were ever taken away, the universe itself would collapse. (*LIG* 255)

In *Collected Stories* alone, forty-two separate fictional worlds emerge individually and then combine to produce small galaxies within the whole cosmos of the volume. In fact, that paradoxical condition of successful existence both alone and in combination with other elements represents the essence of intertextuality as Faulkner handles it in each phase of his career. The children of "That Evening Sun," for example, have the same names as three of the Compson children in *The Sound and the Fury*, and Quentin Compson stands at the center of *Absalom, Absalom!*. What then should we make of the facts that

Quentin's first appearance in Faulkner's fiction finds him committing suicide at age nineteen, that *Absalom* cites his age as twenty, and that he appears as a twenty-four-year-old narrator in "That Evening Sun"? How should we interpret Benjy's absence from the short story or Caddy's absence from *Absalom*? We could take Faulkner's advice from the prefatory note to *The Mansion* and just overlook such differences, but that seems too facile an explanation for them. Just because he said that he knew the characters better than he used to does not mean that we do. However, we can look at what his omissions and additions tell us about how his imagination solved the individual problems of the work at hand. For instance, a 33-year-old Benjy with the mind of a three-year-old opens a novel about the difficulty of expression and interpretation. But a three-year-old Benjy could offer nothing to the action of "That Evening Sun," in which three children at different stages of cognitive ability are trying to figure out their places in the world. What seems to remain constant among the characters' various appearances in texts is their essential personalities, the means by which we recognize and come to understand people – bravery, passivity, kindness, curiosity, spunk, indecisiveness, greed, pure meanness. Faulkner's short stories bring those and other traits into sharp and immediate focus, in what he called "the most demanding form after poetry" (*LIG* 217).

Nonfiction

Faulkner wrote and published nonfiction from the time he began to write for the Ole Miss newspaper *The Mississippian* until the end of his career. This nonfiction includes book and theater reviews, letters to editors of magazines and newspapers, commissioned articles, speeches, introductions to his own works, and essays on topics of the day. As the editor of the most comprehensive edition of the nonfiction explains, those pieces have the same remarkable variety that distinguishes his fiction. He adds:

> One can also learn a great deal about William Faulkner's intelligence, knowledge, imagination, talent, and sense of humor by observing in the differences of any one speech from all the others not only the variety of his interests and the strength of his beliefs but also how aware he is of his particular audience and of how he appears to that audience.
>
> (*ESPL* x–xi)

His nonfiction work, then, shows longstanding concerns with narrative strategies and anxiety about communicating the subtlety of any given idea to an audience.

Subtlety is not a word generally associated with the public expression of ideas, but it perfectly captures Faulkner's approach to such occasions. That subtlety could appear in the form of humor, as it does in "A Guest's Impression of New England" when he describes a visit to Malcolm Cowley's home turf, or "An Innocent at Rinkside," a piece that *Sports Illustrated* commissioned on his impressions of a hockey game. In the former, having stopped to ask whether a road crosses a certain mountain, Cowley drives on but then returns to ask, "Can I get over it in this car?" and his guide says, "No . . . I dont think you can." Faulkner interprets this exchange as typical of "the New Englander, who respects your right to privacy and free will by telling, giving you only and exactly what you asked for, and no more" (*ESPL* 45–6). In the latter Faulkner interrupts his meditation on the appeal of the game to "wonder just what a professional hockey-match, whose purpose is to make a decent and reasonable profit for its owners, had to do with our National Anthem" (*ESPL* 51). His wit could turn from the specific barb to its implications for American culture, or he could become contemplative, as he does in his essays on his impressions of places such as Japan, which he visited on behalf of the State Department in 1955 (*ESPL* 76–81). He articulated reasoned and sincere explanations of race relations in the South; he bitterly criticized his homeland for the murder of Emmett Till and equally remonstrated against forced integration by the North. He offered earnest cultural critique, particularly in the context of advice to young writers, as he did when he spoke to the English Club at the University of Virginia in 1958. He began by explaining President Dwight Eisenhower's People-to-People Program, which tried to get groups of people in the United States "to speak to their individual opposite numbers all over the earth" (*ESPL* 160). Faulkner criticized the idea not for its effort at global communication but for its emphasis on group membership as the only legitimate basis of human interaction, an emphasis that existed because of "an evil inherent in our culture itself," "the mystical belief, almost a religion, that individual man cannot speak to individual man because individual man can no longer exist" (*ESPL* 161). He advised the young writers in the group "to save mankind from being desouled as the stallion or boar or bull is gelded; to save the individual from anonymity before it is too late and humanity has vanished from the animal called man" (*ESPL* 165).

Similar sentiments appear in his most famous piece of nonfiction, the address he delivered in Stockholm upon receiving the Nobel Prize for Literature in 1950. Given yearly in recognition of a writer's entire body of work – rather than for a single text, like the Pulitzer Prize or National Book Award – the Nobel confirmed Faulkner as a literary star in the international firmament. He began his speech by noting that he could easily "find a dedication for the money part of it commensurate with the purpose and significance of its origin" (*ESPL* 119). He did so by establishing scholarship funds for a variety of students, including the black folk of Lafayette County. He said that his speech would "do the same with the acclaim too, by using this moment as a pinnacle from which I might be listened to by the young men and women already dedicated to the same anguish and travail" of writing, "among whom is already that one who will some day stand here where I am standing" (*ESPL* 119). He began his exhortation in an odd place, with an acknowledgment of life in a postnuclear world: "There is only the question: When will I be blown up?" He faced the issue of physical terror by noting that "the basest of all things is to be afraid," and "basest" might well mean in this context not only "lowest" or "least important" but also "most basic." If everyone fears something, he said, then "forget it forever" and concentrate on responses to fear: "the old verities and truths of the heart, the old universal truths lacking which any story is ephemeral and doomed – love and honor and pity and pride and compassion and sacrifice" (*ESPL* 120). The writer who does not heed this advice "writes not of love but of lust, of defeats in which nobody loses anything of value, of victories without hope," and "His griefs grieve on no universal bones, leaving no scars. He writes not of the heart but of the glands" (120).

Some commentators have read those lines as Faulkner's indictment of his own novels. In the context of the speech, though, it is clear that Faulkner cautions against the kind of doomsday literature that a writer fixed on the atom bomb as a metaphor for modern life might create – a *Howl* by Allen Ginsberg, for instance. Rather, Faulkner says, in the postapocalyptic world "when the last ding-dong of doom has clanged and faded from the last worthless rock hanging tideless in the last red and dying evening," man will not be apparent only because of "his puny inexhaustible voice, still talking." "I believe," he said, "that man will not only endure: he will prevail":

> He is immortal, not because he alone among creatures has an inexhaustible voice, but because he has a soul, a spirit capable of compassion and sacrifice and endurance. The poet's, the writer's, duty is to write about these things. It is his privilege to help man endure by lifting his heart, by reminding him of the courage and honor and hope and pride and compassion and pity and sacrifice which have been the glory of his past. The poet's voice need not merely be the record of man, it can be one of the props, the pillars to help him endure and prevail.   (*ESPL* 120)

The writer of this speech values the living gesture made in the face of sure oblivion. The same writer wrote fictions full of such gestures, large and small:

Lena Grove traveling with her baby; Shreve "playing too" in the details of the Sutpen story; Sarty Snopes trudging into the breaking day; Rider crying tears as big as marbles; Mannie Hait frying ham in the barn; Wash Jones running toward the arresting posse with a scythe. That writer, like Shakespeare and Whitman before him, contained contradictory multitudes and, to our everlasting benefit, he recorded the various struggles, reconciliations, and impasses he saw between them – fictional and nonfictional subjects alike. He left us nothing less than the history of his own multifaceted imagination.

Chapter 3

Contexts

William Faulkner remarked on more than one occasion that he was a farmer, not a literary man (*LIG* 59, 169, 234). "I wonder," he wrote to a young woman in 1953, "if you have ever had that thought about the work and the country man whom you know as Bill Faulkner – what little connection there seems to be between them"; in the same letter he marveled at "the amazing gift I had: uneducated in every formal sense, without even very literate, let alone literary, companions, yet to have made the things I made" (*SL* 348). Such poses, combined with his self-deprecating sense of humor, obscure the vibrant intellectual life he actually lived. During his three years as postmaster at the University of Mississippi branch in Oxford, for example, when he would not distribute magazines to patrons until he had finished reading them, he had access to and obviously read an eclectic range of magazines, from numbers of *The Dial* containing T. S. Eliot's *The Waste Land* in 1922 to the first issue of *Time* in 1923. He had an intense few years of reading and study with Phil Stone, jobs in bookstores and bookkeeping in New York and New Haven, and travels to Europe, New Orleans, and the Mississippi Gulf Coast during which he continued to absorb the ideas of his day and test them against the people he observed. And those instances are drawn only from the first twenty-five years of his life. For his entire career Faulkner would remain deeply engaged with the literary, historical, and contemporary contexts in which he found himself, and his fiction reflects that engagement.

His early imagination responded first to the Victorian poets. He loved the poetry of Algernon Charles Swinburne and A. E. Housman, neither of whom is very popular today. In Swinburne, Faulkner heard the world-weary tone of the decadent man tired of life:

> From too much love of living,
> From hope and fear set free,
> We thank with brief thanksgiving
> Whatever gods may be
> That no life lives forever;

> That dead men rise up never;
> That even the weariest river
>   Winds somewhere safe to sea.[1]

In Housman he met "the Shropshire lad," a persona through whom the poet spoke in order to create the illusion of distance between himself and the emotions of his subject matter. The most well-known of his poems today is "To an Athlete Dying Young" (1896), its subject typical of Housman's poetry:

> Now you will not swell the rout
> Of lads that wore their honors out,
> Runners whom renown outran
> And the name died before the man.
>
> So set, before its echoes fade,
> The fleet foot on the sill of shade,
> And hold to the low lintel up
> The still defended challenge cup.[2]

Life was gorgeous, worth savoring fully, but doomed to die. At the age of twenty-eight, Faulkner described the effect these two poets had on him: "At the age of sixteen, I discovered Swinburne. Or rather, Swinburne discovered me"; "It seems to me now that I found him nothing but a flexible vessel into which I might put my own vague emotional shapes without breaking them."[3] He added that Housman "was reason for being born into a fantastic world: discovering the splendor of fortitude, the beauty of being of the soil like a tree about which fools might howl and which winds of disillusion and despair might strip, leaving it bleak, without bitterness; beautiful in sadness." He added that these two poets brought him to Shakespeare and the Elizabethan poets and then to an appreciation of the Romantic poets John Keats and Percy Bysshe Shelley: "That beautiful awareness, so sure of its own power that it is not necessary to create the illusion of force by frenzy and motion," "the spiritual beauty which the moderns strive vainly for with trickery" (*EPP* 117). He concluded his tribute with a call for "among us a Keats in embryo, someone who will tune his lute to the beauty of the world":

> Life is not different from what it was when Shelley drove like a swallow
> southward from the unbearable English winter; living may be different,
> but not life. Time changes us, but Time's self does not change. Here is
> the same air, the same sunlight in which Shelley dreamed of golden men
> and women immortal in a silver world . . . Is not there among us
> someone who can write something beautiful and passionate and sad
> instead of saddening?   (*EPP* 118)

In his opinion, he was that poet. He wrote to his mother from Paris that same year, "I have just written such a beautiful thing that I am about to bust – 2000 words about the Luxembourg Gardens and death." He mentions its "thin thread of a plot, about a young woman" and calls it "poetry though written in prose form" (*SL* 17). Taken with the printed reminiscence, the description anticipates the ending of *Sanctuary* (1931), where Temple Drake, her face "sullen and discontented and sad," listens to a band in the Luxembourg Gardens and follows the music "across the pool and the opposite semicircle of trees where at somber intervals the dead tranquil queens in stained marble mused, and on into the sky lying prone and vanquished in the embrace of the season of rain and death" (317). There is an unmistakable debt in the closing lines of one of his most nihilistic novels, a direct line to the poets he admired as an adolescent and young man.

Faulkner also greatly admired the poetry of the French Symbolists of the late nineteenth century. From them he learned how to invest an object with layered and multiple meanings – generally on the topics of lost or impossible love and death – and to approach his subject matter indirectly. Two examples from his early poetry written after the manner of Paul Verlaine illustrate these lessons. In the first a moonlit garden stands for a woman's troubled soul; in the second a poplar tree becomes a young girl on the verge of her first sexual experience:

> In the calm moonlight, so lovely fair
> That makes the birds dream in the slender trees,
> While fountains dream among the statues there;
> Slim fountains sob in silver ecstasies.   (*EPP* 58)

> You are a young girl
> Trembling in the throes of ecstatic modesty,
> A white objective girl
> Whose clothing has been forcibly taken away from her.   (*EPP* 60)

The last line of the second example at first seems clunky and awkward, but on examination the poet's pity for the frightened virgin begins to emerge; her trembling does not necessarily do romantic credit to the person causing it. Such ambivalence in interpretive matters would come to mark Faulkner's fiction, as it does in the scene in *Light in August* (1932) that describes Joe Christmas after his castration, with "something, a shadow, about his mouth" and in dying "soaring into their memories forever and ever" (464–5). Faulkner's sympathy with objects of sexual desire would manifest itself in characters such as Caddy Compson in *The Sound and the Fury* (1929), whose family members each demand something of her as she matures and so objectify her for their own purposes. She, like the poplar lady, never speaks a word to us. In the first example above, Faulkner (then writing as Falkner) sounds words over and over, lining them up with other words and repeating them to musical effect, again with a jarring ending: the "Slim fountains sob," but in "silver ecstasies" that literally reflect the moonlight of the stanza's first line. In such works we see Faulkner learning to load images not just land with symbolic meaning but with music and rhythm. Some of the most famous lines from *Light in August* show how well he learned that lesson: "with sparrowlike childtrebling, orphans in identical and uniform blue denim in and out of remembering but in knowing constant as the bleak walls, the bleak windows where in rain soot from the yearly adjacenting chimneys streaked like black tears" (119). Not only does he make new words to contain the musical quality of the children's voices, he also builds in definite meter toward the final sad image of "black tears," itself a perfect yet indirectly articulated symbol of Joe Christmas's agonized life.

As powerful as those early encounters with the poets were, Faulkner chose the path of serious fiction, and as a denizen of the twentieth-century literary world, he had to contend with the giants of his time. These were without question the poet T. S. Eliot and the novelist James Joyce. *The Waste Land* and *Ulysses* appeared in the same year, and in 1923 Eliot published an analysis of Joyce's novel that would become perhaps as influential as the novel itself. In it he explained how Joyce had used contemporary characters to retrace the paths taken by Odysseus, Telemachus, and Penelope in Homer's *Odyssey*. In doing so he had discovered "a way of controlling, of ordering, of giving a shape and a significance to the immense panorama of futility and anarchy which is contemporary history."[4] Eliot's *The Waste Land* did precisely that:

> What are the roots that clutch, what branches grow
> Out of this stony rubbish? Son of man,
> You cannot say, or guess, for you know only
> A heap of broken images, where the sun beats,
> And the dead tree gives no shelter, the cricket no relief,
> And the dry stone no sound of water.[5]

This passage gives readers a clue to how to read the poem; it is a "heap of broken images," various voices juxtaposed with one another with no apparent "roots" or ultimate meaning. As disparaging as his early assessment of the "trickery" practiced by modern poets was, Faulkner absorbed Eliot's work. His novel *Pylon* (1935) refers directly and indirectly to "The Love Song of J. Alfred Prufrock" (1917) and *The Waste Land*; he entitled one section of *Collected Stories*

(1950) "The Waste Land"; imagery from Eliot's poetry permeates Quentin's section of *The Sound and the Fury* (1929); and his first novel portrays the "futility and anarchy which is contemporary history" for the survivors of the Great War. Joyce had an equally strong effect on Faulkner, particularly as an innovator of prose. Widely credited with introducing stream-of-consciousness narration to fiction, Joyce had also written exclusively about what he might have called his own "postage stamp of native soil," his native Ireland, in spite of the fact that he had left it permanently at the age of twenty-two. Faulkner would also choose to immerse himself in his native land to find his art. In fact, in the early review quoted above, he said that by choosing to remain in the South "all contact, saving by the printed word, with contemporary poets is impossible" (*EPP* 116). Of course, "the printed word" is how he knew Eliot and Joyce and how the literary world would come to know him. How Joyce used the printed word fascinated him; from him Faulkner learned "portmanteau words," words that compounded other words into new meaning, like "childtrebling" in *Light in August*. He also saw in *Ulysses* extended examples of shifting narrative perspective and stream-of-consciousness in simultaneous action. Here is Leopold Bloom, Joyce's Odysseus/Ulysses, trying to avoid someone on the street:

> I am looking for that, Yes, that. Try all pockets. Handker, *Freeman*. Where did I?
> Ah, yes, Trousers. Purse. Potato. Where did I?
> Hurry, Walk quietly, Moment more. My heart.
> His hand looking for the where did I put found in his hip pocket soap lotion have to call tepid paper stuck. Ah, soap there! Yes. Gate.
> Safe![6]

Moving into and out of Bloom's thoughts, the narrator steps outside of conventional narrative forms and makes new ones to represent the modern reality through which Bloom moves. Faulkner would do exactly that, from the free-floating perspective of *Mosquitoes* (1927) to the named dramatic monologue chapters of *As I Lay Dying* (1930) to the assembled episodes of *Go Down, Moses* (1942) to the framed reminiscence of *The Reivers* (1962).

Unlike Eliot, Faulkner did not despair of contemporary history. Instead, more like Joyce, he kept very close track of it and of the ways in which men and women chose to interpret it. His fiction records a range of responses to the major wars of his day, for example. The Civil War that shaped his South and his America figures prominently in "Mountain Victory," "Wash," "There Was a Queen," *Flags in the Dust/Sartoris* (1929), *Light in August, Absalom, Absalom!* (1936), *The Unvanquished* (1938), and *Go Down, Moses*. The Great

War stands at the center of *Soldiers' Pay* (1926) and most of the stories in "The Waste Land" section of *Collected Stories*, and the Second World War shapes the lives of characters in *Go Down, Moses, Intruder in the Dust* (1948), and the last two volumes of the Snopes trilogy. Those latter two books and certain of his nonfiction pieces reveal a sophisticated understanding of Cold War politics and of the potentially devastating effects of man's increasing reliance on technology. His Nobel Prize speech, for instance, cites the "universal physical fear" of getting "blown up" in the nuclear age as nothing less than "Our tragedy today" (*ESPL* 119); and he once wrote a letter to the editor of the *New York Times* decrying "that mystical, unquestioning, almost religious awe and veneration in which our culture has trained us to hold gadgets – any gadget, if it is only complex enough and cryptic enough and costs enough" (*ESPL* 213).

The arena in which Faulkner strived most mightily to affect the course of contemporary history was the most incendiary of his time. Faulkner shared some of the racial prejudices of whites in his region, but he came to see those prejudices as self-delusional and unjust; indeed, his fiction is ahead of its time in representing the warping effects of racist ideology. During the fledgling years of the American civil rights movement, he spoke and published on issues of race relations that satisfied almost none of the parties interested in them. He stood against forced integration even as he supported equality of opportunity and status before the law for black people. His advice that the North "go slow" with integration in the South (*ESPL* 87) resulted in a challenge to debate from the black intellectual and activist W. E. B. Du Bois, which Faulkner refused in a telegram to the *New York Times*: "I DO NOT BELIEVE THERE IS A DEBATABLE POINT BETWEEEN US." he cabled; Du Bois was right "MORALLY LEGALLY AND ETHICALLY," but he was right "PRACTICALLY" (*SL* 398). He spoke out in the *New York Herald Tribune* against the murder of fourteen-year-old Emmett Till, allegedly for whistling at a white woman:

> Perhaps the purpose of this sorry and tragic error committed in my
> native Mississippi by two white adults on an afflicted Negro child is to
> prove to us whether or not we deserve to survive. Because if we in
> America have reached that point in our desperate culture when we must
> murder children, no matter for what reason or what color, we don't
> deserve to survive, and probably won't.   (*ESPL* 223)[7]

Such commentary infuriated the reactionary white citizens of the South and elsewhere, resulting in what he called "so much threatening fan mail, so many nut angry telephone calls at 2 and 3 am from that country, that maybe I'll come over to the Delta to test them" (*SL* 388). He kept trying to be heard, however, going so far as to give a speech at the University of Virginia in 1958 calling for

Virginians to lead the rest of the South in removing barriers between white people and "a minority as large as ten per cent held second class in citizenship by the accident of physical appearance" (*ESPL* 155). That speech contains some astute observations on the psychology of American race relations:

> It is possible that the white race and the Negro race can never really like and trust each other; this for the reason that the white man can never really know the Negro, because the white man has forced the Negro to be always a Negro rather than another human being in their dealings, and therefore the Negro cannot afford, does not dare, to be open with the white man and let him know what he, the Negro, thinks. But I do know that we in the South, having grown up with and lived among Negroes for generations, are capable in individual cases of liking and trusting individual Negroes, which the North can never do because the northerner only fears him.   (*ESPL* 157)

More than one African American writer has spoken to that truth, from Du Bois in *The Souls of Black Folk* (1903) in his analysis of the double-consciousness of the person born both black and American, to Richard Wright describing the fear that Bigger Thomas both feels and generates in *Native Son* (1940). Far from listening to Faulkner, the state of Virginia closed two public schools later that year rather than integrate them.

Faulkner also habitually kept a close eye on contemporary political events and social phenomena, and both his private correspondence and his public utterances reflect his interests. He wrote letters to editors of newspapers and magazines to criticize the hit-and-run driver that killed one of his dogs, to praise a jury that convicted white men for killing black children, to support the preservation of the Oxford courthouse, to wish that he had written *Moll Flanders* (1722) *Moby-Dick* (1851), and *When We Were Very Young* (1924), and to speak in favor of legalizing beer. He wrote a thoughtful letter to his stepson supporting his decision to enlist during the Second World War, and five months later he wrote similarly to his nephew, a pilot, sending him a good-luck talisman and recalling his own "crack-up in '18," which never happened (*SL* 166, 170). As his story "Golden Land" corroborates, he also drew an early and accurate bead on the fakery of Hollywood: "the moving picture people, and the real estate agents and lawyers and merchants and all the other parasites who exist only because of motion picture salaries, including the fake doctors and faith-healers and swamis and blackmailing private detectives who live on the people who draw motion picture salaries" (*SL* 165). For several years he drew motion picture salaries himself as a scriptwriter: "I am well and quite busy," he wrote to his friend and publisher, "surrounded by snow, dogs, Indians, Red Coats, and

Nazi spies" (*SL* 167). He wrote bitterly of that friend's son's death in the war and of a group of black folks killed by a mob in Detroit even as a squadron of black pilots distinguished itself in service: "if the politicians and the people who run this country are not forced to make good the shibboleth they glibly talk about freedom, liberty, human rights, then you young men who live through it will have wasted your precious time, and those who dont live through it will have died in vain" (*SL* 176). Such concern with the world around him also marks the pages of his fiction. For example, he knew how to make shingles and how to use a froe, as "Shingles for the Lord" demonstrates. "The Tail Men" registers his awareness of how the country's first peacetime draft divided the populace. A popular brand of condoms makes it into the pages of *The Sound and the Fury* (50), and a telephone operator's affected nasal accent graces *Sanctuary*: "Pine Bluff dizzent. . . . Enkyew!" (that is, "Pine Bluff doesn't answer, thank you!") (269). Such details reflect the writer's keen observation of his contemporary scene.

There is another, specifically literary context in which to understand the career of this writer from the South, and that is in relation to his contemporaries. When asked in 1947 to rank his accomplishments among those of other writers of his time, Faulkner placed himself second behind Thomas Wolfe, author of *Look Homeward, Angel* (1929), and ahead of John Dos Passos (*USA* [1938]), Ernest Hemingway, and John Steinbeck. What he said about Hemingway made that writer furious: "has no courage, has never climbed out on a limb. He has never used a word where the reader might check his usage by a dictionary" (*LIG* 58). Hemingway took this as an aspersion on his character. Faulkner meant it as criticism of his craftsmanship, as he explained in an interview in 1955:

> I rated Wolfe first, myself second. I put Hemingway last. I said we were all failures. All of us had failed to match the dream of perfection and I rated the authors on the basis of their splendid failure to do the impossible. I believed Wolfe tried to do the greatest of the impossible, that he tried to reduce all human experience to literature. And I thought that after Wolfe I had tried the most. I rated Hemingway last because he stayed within what he knew. He did it fine, but he didn't try for the impossible.   (*LIG* 81)

It is more helpful to try to discern what these writers had in common that would lead Faulkner to group them together than to focus solely on his rankings. Over the years he also expressed admiration for Willa Cather (*My Ántonia* [1918], *Death Comes for the Archbishop* [1927]), Erskine Caldwell (*Tobacco Road* [1932], *God's Little Acre* [1933]), and Thomas Mann, and he greatly admired Anita Loos's *Gentlemen Prefer Blondes* (1925) and sent her his "envious congratulations on Dorothy," its spunky brunette antiheroine (*SL* 32). He always appreciated well-done humor. The other writers in this group tended either to recreate specific regions and their inhabitants – like Cather's Nebraska and Caldwell's poor white southerners – or to stretch toward prose innovations. Hemingway certainly did the latter, with his famous dicta about stripping away adjectives and adverbs and leaving most of the meaning of his fiction submerged below the surface of the text. He certainly revolutionized the representation of dialogue, particularly in his short stories, and his greatest novels appeared alongside Faulkner's for virtually all of their simultaneous careers. They published their first novels in 1926 (*The Sun Also Rises* and *Soldiers' Pay*); *A Farewell to Arms* came out in the same year as *The Sound and the Fury*; *For Whom the Bell Tolls* (1940) and *Go Down, Moses* appeared within two years of one another. Faulkner won the Nobel Prize in 1950, Hemingway in 1953. These two polar opposites – the blustery midwesterner and reticent southerner, the writer of spare prose and the writer of the longest sentences in American fiction – were each other's most significant contemporaries. Their mutual successes in fiction writing give but one indication of the robust quality of American literature in the twentieth century.

Faulkner could also spot and would occasionally encourage talented younger writers, the audience he targeted in his Nobel Prize address. He spoke highly of Eudora Welty and Ralph Ellison, and he wrote to Richard Wright that he "said it well" in *Black Boy* (1945), Wright's scathing autobiography, but that "I think you said it much better in *Native Son* [1940]" (*SL* 201). He was sympathetic to black writers because of the "terrible burden that the Negro has to carry in my country":

> I think it implies a very fine talent, that it is strong enough so that he can accept the fact that he is a Negro and then stop worrying about it and be a writer. Much more difficult than the white man [who] hasn't got that pressure on him all the time to remind him what he is by the color of his skin, by social condition, by status. (*ESPL* 185–6)

Then again, after his own success, he cast a giant shadow on the literary landscape. As Flannery O'Connor, a gifted writer from Georgia, put it, "The presence alone of Faulkner in our midst makes a great difference in what the writer can and cannot permit himself to do. Nobody wants his mule and wagon stalled on the same track the Dixie Limited is roaring down."[8] Twelve years before Toni Morrison won her own Nobel Prize, she gave an interview in which she discussed the worlds made by the great fiction writers before her:

> I never asked Tolstoy to write for me, a little colored girl in Lorain, Ohio. I never asked Joyce not to mention Catholicism or the world of Dublin. Never. And I don't know why I should be asked to explain your life to you. We have splendid writers to do that, but I am not one of them. It is that business of being universal, a word hopelessly stripped of meaning for me. Faulkner wrote what I suppose could be called regional literature and had it published all over the world. It is good – and universal – because it is specifically about a particular world. That's what I wish to do.[9]

Making "a particular world" sums up the achievement of the writers William Faulkner most admired and those to whom he compared his own. He said that he read "the Old Testament, Dickens, Conrad, Cervantes . . . Flaubert, Balzac – he created an intact world of his own, a bloodstream running through twenty books – Dostoevsky, Tolstoi, Shakespeare" and Herman Melville, among prose writers. In the same interview he took up the anti-intellectual pose when asked if he had read Freud: "Everybody talked about Freud when I lived in New Orleans, but I have never read him. Neither did Shakespeare. I doubt if Melville did either, and I'm sure Moby Dick didn't" (*LIG* 251). Five months before he received the news of his Nobel Prize, he had written to the American Academy of Arts and Letters to accept the William Dean Howells medal, awarded only every five years. In that acceptance lies a melancholy assessment of his career:

> None of mine ever suited me, each time I wrote the last word I would think, if I could just do it over, I would do it better, maybe even right. But I was too busy; there was always another one, I would tell myself. Maybe I'm too young or busy to decide: when I reach fifty, I will be able to decide how good or not. Then one day I was fifty and I looked back at it, and I decided that it was all pretty good – and then in the same instant I realised that that was the worst of all since that meant only that a little nearer now was the moment, instant, *night*: dark: sleep: when I would put it all away forever that I anguished and sweated over, and it would never trouble me anymore. (*ESPL* 206)

Twelve years would elapse between that letter and the moment he "put it all away forever," but his work and the contexts in which it appears remain central to a full understanding of American literature and, indeed, American life and culture.

That is quite a position for "an old veteran sixth-grader" (*ESPL* 219) to occupy.

Chapter 4

Critical reception

With the exception of another William, Faulkner has now generated more published commentary than any other writer, and that one's last name is Shakespeare. During his lifetime, Faulkner developed a few strategies for dealing with critics and with criticism. He usually ignored it, but when he could not he tended to agree with it and add his own. When Malcolm Cowley was preparing the *Portable Faulkner* (1946), for example, Faulkner wrote, "I'll go further than you in the harsh criticism. The style, as you divine, is a result of the solitude, and granted a bad one" (*SL* 215). To an English professor who had sent him three essays, Faulkner sent his thanks and added, "I agree with them. You found implications which I had missed," partly because "I am an old 8th grade man." Yet when he closed the letter with "Excuse all the I's. I'm still having trouble reconciling method and material, you see," he as much as told the professor to take a hike (*SL* 142–3). The prefatory note to *The Mansion* (1959) says that "the author has already found more discrepancies and contradictions than he hopes the reader will" and serves as yet another reminder that Faulkner and not professional critics held sway in the worlds of his creation. Yet he wrote to be read, and one of his earliest critics noted a quality that readers still prize in his work, "a game in which he displays tremendous ingenuity and gives pleasure to the reader by stimulating a like ingenuity on his part."[1] In the spirit of stimulating such like ingenuity, this chapter, in conjunction with the "Guide to further reading," intends to help beginning readers of the criticism through its sometimes treacherous waters.

The careers of writers depend at first on published reviews of their work. A good review in a prestigious newspaper or journal can boost sales, and some writers think that even a bad review in a prominent place is better than no notice at all. From the beginning of his career, Faulkner got good, bad, and indifferent notices in publications large and small. This happened partly because his writing was difficult to understand, but it also happened because of the literary climate of the day, in which reviewers tended to be either humanist in their preferences or leftist. The former prized novels with "spiritual resonance," the latter calls to political action to improve the world. Neither got what they wanted from novels like *As I Lay Dying* (1930) and *Sanctuary* (1931). Faulkner was early on described as "abnormally fond of morons, idiots, perverts, and nymphomaniacs," "the leading member of a 'cult of cruelty'" (Hoffman 2) – a view that persists in some quarters today. One writer has characterized the patterns of Faulkner's reviews as follows:

> in the 1920's, Faulkner was scarcely known and indifferently reviewed; in the period from 1929 to 1932 . . . he was given much attention, but it was hesitant and puzzled when not downright indignant; after 1946, the date of the *Portable*, each new Faulkner publication was recognized widely and some effort made to consider it in the light of past achievement.   (Hoffman 15)

To understand the writer's point, consider the following selected comments. *Soldiers' Pay* (1926) was either "Honest but slap-dash" or there had been "no first novel of such magnificent achievement in the last thirty years." The author of *Sartoris* (1929) "could easily lead the pack that helps the *Saturday Evening Post* sell mouthwash to 50 million Americans" or "was one of a very few to whom the term *genius* could be applied." Serious Faulkner criticism began with a pamphlet issued at the time of *The Sound and the Fury* (1929), and reviewers found both artistry in technique and "pathological delinquency" in its pages. One reader found *As I Lay Dying* "precise and vivid" while others bemoaned its "content" and "pageant of degeneracy." Clifton Fadiman, the most acerbic of Faulkner's critics, found *Sanctuary* "a calculated assault on one's sense of the normal" and said of *Absalom, Absalom!* (1936) that "every person in [it] comes to no good end, and they all take a hell of a time coming even that far"; Faulkner's style in the latter novel he called the "Non-stop or Life Sentence" (Hoffman 15–20). Famous writers also weighed in on Faulkner throughout his career, with just as varied opinions. André Malraux described *Sanctuary* as "the intrusion of Greek tragedy into the detective story."[2] Allen Tate called Faulkner "the greatest American novelist after Henry James" of "an originality and power not equaled by his contemporaries, Hemingway and Fitzgerald." The British novelist Graham Greene said that *Absalom* contained "fake poetry" and "pseudo-tragic talk of doom and fate and the furies"; several attributed severe misogyny and racism to Faulkner; Eudora Welty praised him for the way "the humor is born" in his stories, "as much their blood and bones as the passion and the poetry," and Albert Camus called him "your greatest writer" and "one of the rare creators of the West" (Warren 274–95).

Virtually all of the assessments of Faulkner's career as a whole try to explain the huge increase in his visibility and popularity after winning the Nobel Prize in 1950. One critic rightly notes that the process of "bringing him to a position of deserved reputation" began in 1939 and accelerated with Cowley's edition of *The Portable Faulkner* for Viking Press in 1946. "The effect of the prize," he claims, "was to bring him 'up front,' to make a 'public man' of him, and to exert such pressure upon the general run of critics and journalists that they could not thereafter dismiss him out of hand"; "the prize discouraged some critics and frightened others into confessions of their past errors" (Hoffman 26). Robert Penn Warren was one of the first to note Faulkner's "canonization" in the 1950s and 1960s by a "cult" of admirers: "it is well to recall that the snobbery of the cult merges with the snobbery of the academy, and that the process of exegesis has contributed to the sense that only by the application of academic method and in the exfoliation of theses can the truth be found, be packaged, and be delivered for consumption" (Warren 20). In other words, Faulkner mattered because college professors said that he did, and they set themselves up as the conduit between his meaning and the reading public. Faulkner had resisted that very commodification when the University of Mississippi issued a press release with comments he made during some English classes he addressed there in 1947. Among them was his assessment of Ernest Hemingway as a writer with "no courage." Faulkner had reviewed the instructor's notes and given "the English department, not the publicity department" permission to make use of them. The publicity department used them anyway, doing exactly what Faulkner had said he would "resist with my last breath"; "the high-pressure ballyhoo which even universities now believe they must employ: the damned eternal American BUY! BUY!! BUY!!! 'Try us first, our campus covers ONE WHOLE SQUARE MILE, you can see our water tank from twelve miles away, our football team almost beat A&M, we have WM FAULKNER at 6 (count them: 6) English classes'" (*SL* 249). So began the literal critical fortune that would increase almost exponentially after the Nobel Prize, and here, too, was his resistance to being packaged and sold.

Attempts to assess Faulkner's career after the Nobel Prize have also noted that between *Go Down, Moses* (1942) and the Prize he published only one novel and one collection of short stories (*Intruder in the Dust* [1948] and *Knight's Gambit* [1949]). During that period he struggled with the writing of *A Fable*, which preoccupied him from 1943 until its publication in 1954. During those years, a character came to prominence in Faulkner's fiction whom the critics almost universally read as "Faulkner's spokesman" and also almost universally despised. The lawyer Gavin Stevens, who had been demonstrably wrong about his interpretation of events in *Light in August* (1932) and *Go Down, Moses*, appeared in *Intruder* as a long-winded commentator on America's racial problems and in *Requiem for a Nun* (1951) as Temple Drake Stevens's opinionated interlocutor. It seems that because Gavin was a well-meaning middle-aged white southerner and Faulkner was a middle-aged white south-erner whose Nobel Prize speech had voiced faith that "man will prevail," critics took Gavin's rhetoric for Faulkner's and insisted that the character spoke for the man and his region. The critics almost immediately characterized their own transference as Faulkner's "preaching." In addition, Faulkner made many public appearances after the Prize, invited by various groups including the US State Department, at which he was treated as a spokesman for art, especially art in America. A shy and private man, he hated that role, but he tried to live up to its demands. He did so in part by relying on some preformulated ideas and phrases that could help him through often repeated questions and requests for comment. His public comments were lined up against his fiction, and neither fared well by comparison. "Much of the criticism of the 1940's was concerned with the developmental strategies of Faulkner's writings," says Frederick Hoffman, but in the 1950s it became focused on their "moral mean-ings," particularly the implicit Christian ones (Hoffman 31). The criticism of his work shifted, then, from condemning him as a pagan to celebrating him as a humanist.

For an intense few years, then, a great many Faulkner scholars began the hunt for Christ in his pages, and especially after the publication of *A Fable*, they did not have to look far. Benjy Compson celebrates his thirty-third birthday during Easter weekend in *The Sound and the Fury*; Joe Christmas is lynched at the age of thirty-three in *Light in August*; a squad of twelve men led by a nameless corporal tries to stop war in *A Fable*, and the corporal is exe-cuted between two thieves. This kind of critical activity drove one writer to this:

> When Faulkner writes a novel,
> He crowds his symbols in;
> There is a hidden meaning
> In every glass of gin,
>
> In every maiden ravished,
> In every colt that's foaled,
> And specially in characters
> That are thirty-three years old.   (Hoffman 35)

This drive to find faith in Faulkner's novels continues to some extent in con-temporary criticism, but recent writers tend to remain content with Faulkner's own repeated description of his use of Christian motifs: "that was a tool" (*FIU* 68).

What continues to interest critics is how he used his tools and, in another paradigm shift in Faulkner studies, how his tools might have used him, or at least escaped his control.[3] Those in the first category include first of all the influential New Critics. This school of criticism began in the 1940s and dominated literary criticism until the 1970s, and its practitioners included some of the most prominent names in an increasingly large field of Faulkner criticism. It relies on close readings of texts in order to discover their meanings, which exist solely in the literary artifact itself and not in social or cultural contexts outside it. Consequently a New Critic looks closely at a work's symbols, motifs, recurring patterns, images, and so forth and then might well move through an author's career to base generalizations about his or her body of work on a series of such readings. This was certainly the case in Faulkner studies in the years immediately after his death, when a canon emerged because he was no longer present to continue changing it by publishing new work. Perhaps not surprisingly, this criticism also became canonized. Almost to a person, the New Critics read Faulkner's career in three phases: the apprenticeship period that produced his first three novels; the "major phase" that ran from *The Sound and the Fury* in 1929 to *Go Down, Moses* in 1942; and the "later phase," the alleged falling-off of his talent during the six years between *Moses* and *Intruder*, which also included the Nobel Prize and his later novels. In effect, the New Critics decided that Faulkner's career had taken the literary equivalent of appearing on the cover of *Sports Illustrated*, that he suffered from what his friend Phil Stone called "Nobelitis in the head" (Blotner 562) and had left his best fiction behind him.

Such readings dominated Faulkner criticism for four decades and continued to plague the scholarship even when correctives to those views began to appear. If the New Critics read Faulkner as a kind of transcendent natural genius, the US government saw him at the same time as someone who could front for American interests on the international literary and diplomatic scene. His reputation was as much a reputation-maker for the government during the Cold War years as it was for those of the New Critics themselves, whose academic careers advanced with each essay and book published and each class taught. There is therefore a good case for reading Faulkner's success as a success for Cold War ideology and for American university politics (though reading Faulkner's fiction of the later years and his nonfiction of the public years does much to temper a hard and fast interpretation along those lines). As new schools of interpretation began to appear, Faulkner's texts – probably because they were already in place in the American literary canon – came in for other kinds of scrutiny and yielded other kinds of rewards for readers. For example, what some early reviewers saw as

Faulkner's discomfort with women and disdain for "weak" men evolved under the lens of gender criticism into his examination of the roles our culture asks us to play because of our biological sex. Temple Drake is not a tease who falls in love with the evil that she cannot help but attract; she is a naïve young woman, ignorant of the real power of sexuality, vicitimized, entrapped, or abandoned by the men of *Sanctuary*, including the ones who should love her. Horace Benbow fails Lee Goodwin in court not because he carries shrimp home every week to his wife but because his sister Narcissa is no better morally than the manipulative legal system that convicts an innocent man. Developments in race theory and studies of ethnicity have led to new ways of viewing the black and racially mixed characters in Faulkner's fiction and his representation of the South as the crucible in which race simmers, reflective of American culture as a whole. Isaac McCaslin's idealization of the wilderness in *Go Down, Moses* thus emerges as a reprehensible retreat from the ethical demands of his family's and his region's history.

Developments in the study of language and its relationship to life have also affected Faulkner scholarship. The New Critics assume a stable text with traceable links between words and meaning, and so do structuralist and narratologist critics. These readers look for what narratives have in common as narratives and for the structural principles operating in a work; then they use those observations to classify texts into types. The interior dramatic monologues that organize *The Sound and the Fury* and *As I Lay Dying* would therefore mark them as distinctively different forms of the novel than the form produced by the free-floating omniscient narrators of *Light in August* and *The Hamlet* (1940). Other readers do not agree with the stability of any given text or the precision of language itself; they point out that language and its meanings change over time, and they believe that it is impossible to find an "original meaning" or "authorial intention" behind a writer's choice of words. Instead, deconstructionist critics read words in relation to one another to find the differences between them, rather than look for a meaning beyond the word itself. A fine example of the deconstructionist's view of language appears in Addie Bundren's chapter of *As I Lay Dying*, in which she claims that words are "just a shape to fill a lack."[4] She thinks of Anse's very name until he deconstructs: "I would think about his name until after a while I could see the word as a shape, a vessel, and I would watch him liquefy and flow into it like cold molasses out of the darkness into a vessel . . . and then I would find that I had forgotten the name of the jar." The same thing happens when she thinks "*Cash* and *Darl* that way until their names would die and solidify into a shape and then fade away" (173):

> And so when Cora Tull would tell me I was not a true mother, I would think how words go straight up in a thin line, quick and harmless, and how terribly doing goes along the earth, clinging to it, so that after a while the two lines are too far apart for the same person to straddle from one to the other; and that sin and love and fear are just sounds that people who never sinned nor loved nor feared have for what they never had and cannot have until they forget the words.   (173–4)

Recognizing the fluidity of language does not have to produce Addie's kind of nihilism about language. It can also introduce the idea of equal worth among multiple voices, indeterminate futures for characters, wordplay, and political heterodoxy. In other words, it can produce literary criticism as flexible as one of Faulkner's fictions. Poststructuralist criticism encompasses just such a variety of approaches to literature, including feminist, Marxist, and the psychoanalytic, to name a few.

Taking a very different tack from scholars focused exclusively on language systems, but just as committed as the poststructuralists to multiple approaches to texts, cultural studies critics look at works in relation to the political, legal, social, and material conditions both of the day that produced them and of the times in which they are read. They do not assume that works of art exist independently of the culture that surrounded the artist; nor do they assume that they interpret in such a vacuum. The rise of cultural studies in many scholarly disciplines is in one sense a symptom of life at the end of the twentieth century and beginning of the twenty-first. Although inequities continue to exist among classes, races, ethnicities, and the sexes and genders, American culture now takes for granted the virtue of diversity. The metaphor of choice to describe that culture is no longer the melting pot but the salad bowl – a combination of ingredients in which the components retain their individual flavors even as they become part of a new whole. Cultural studies of Faulkner have set Dewey Dell's pregnancy in the context of the professionalization of medical fields in the 1920s by men organizing into groups such as the American Medical Association to curtail women's medical practices; they have analyzed the market forces that drove popular magazines such as the *Saturday Evening Post* and consequently affected Faulkner's publication of short stories; they have described what powered the elections of men such as Theodore Bilbo and James K. Vardaman in order to understand the Snopeses; and they have recovered Faulkner's recipe for curing pork.

Beginning readers might well wonder what is the good – or perhaps just the point – of reading or even knowing about such material that they have probably heard loosely described as "literary theory." Much of the criticism exists because professors must usually produce it in order to be hired or promoted. Faulkner's work sits already canonized and validated, needing only a new spin to produce an academic career. Yet even such a cynical explanation does not account for how well Faulkner's texts respond to rigorous intellectual applications of all kinds. *As I Lay Dying*, for example, works as a feminist text when one realizes that Anse's or Moseley's way of looking at women does not help the women at all but instead imprisons them and holds them rather like captive laborers. *The Sound and the Fury* yields new insight when looked at with Freudian eyes. The scariest person in *The Mansion* might not be Flem, who quite naturally does not want to be killed, but Linda, who twice abets his murderer. Interestingly, Faulkner's fiction also looks different when examined by intellectual trends that came after Faulkner produced the work they analyze. For instance, Faulkner will never be a postmodernist, a term initially coined to describe a certain kind of architecture in the 1940s. But that term has evolved to include a mindset that seeks to break down barriers and sees transgression of boundaries as a very valuable human effort. Those senses of postmodernism open interesting windows on novels such as *Requiem for a Nun*, part play and part prose; *If I Forget Thee, Jerusalem* (1939), told in alternating chapters ten years apart chronologically; and *A Fable*, military hierarchy triumphant over all else. Postmodernist thinking can also help us to make sense of a densely poetic story such as "Carcassonne," in which the protagonist has an ongoing conversation with his "skeleton":

> *And me on a buckskin pony with eyes like blue electricity and a mane like tangled fire, galloping up the hill and right off into the high heaven of the world* His skeleton lay still. Perhaps it was thinking about this. Anyway, after a time it groaned. But it said nothing.
>   *which is certainly not like you* he thought *you are not like yourself. but I can't say that a little quiet is not pleasant.*[5]

The protagonist lies in a garret, readying himself for sleep, "beneath an unrolled strip of tarred roofing made of paper. All of him that is, save that part which suffered neither insects nor temperature and which galloped unflagging on the destinationless pony, up a piled silver hill of cumulate where no hoof echoed or left print, toward the blue precipice never gained" (895). Critics have argued that the protagonist is dying, that he is not dying but drifting off to sleep, that he represents a successful artist, that he represents an unsuccessful artist, and so on. The postmodernist critic would not see the importance in deciding such matters but would instead prize the story for its indeterminacy, its refusal to privilege one part of the young man's identity over another, equally important part of it.

All professions have their own specialized terms, which always sound like jargon to those outside the profession. In one sense, then, the -isms described above just give academics a way to talk to one another in shorthand, with a shared vocabulary and sets of assumptions. Yet it would be incorrect to say that the approaches above have no place in a beginning Faulkner reader's experience. All patterns of reading have plans behind them; all syllabi, recommended books, and assignments have something to accomplish. In those ways no reading of anyone's work is without "theory." Even opening a book and reading at random is a kind of plan and produces certain kinds of results. Whether readers of this guide will pursue the criticism further depends on individual tastes, inclinations, and decisions. Understanding that all acts of reading are valuable intellectual exercises, almost whatever the subject matter, is an important step toward becoming a fully developed thinker. At the University of Virginia in 1958, Faulkner said that he for one never read the critics of his own work:

> I'm convinced, though, that that sort of criticism whether it's
> nonsensical or not is valid because it is a symptom of change, of motion,
> which is life, and also it's a proof that literature – art – is a living quantity
> in our social condition. If it were not, then there'd be no reason for
> people to delve and find all sorts of symbolisms and psychological
> strains and currents in it. And I'm quite sure that there are some writers
> to whom that criticism is good, that it could help them find themselves.
> I don't know that the critic could teach the writer anything because I'm
> inclined to think that nobody really can teach anybody anything, that
> you offer it and it's there and if it is your will or urge to learn it you do,
> and the writer that does need the criticism can get quite a lot of benefit
> from it.   (*FIU* 65)

He said that he read books "for fun" and that we should read his books the same way: "read a page or two until you find one that you want to read another page" (*FIU* 64). Reading for him therefore reflected that sense of motion he found characteristic of life, of intellectual change, and of the greatest art – his own included.

Notes

1 Life

1. William Faulkner, *Mosquitoes* (New York: Boni & Liveright, 1927; New York: Pocket Books, 1985), 116–17.

2 Works

1. Ezra Pound, *Hugh Selwyn Mauberly* (1920), in Pound, *Selected Poems of Ezra Pound* (New York: New Directions, 1957), 63–4.
2. William Faulkner, *Soldiers' Pay* (New York: Boni & Liveright, 1926), 231. Further page references will be given parenthetically in the text.
3. William Faulkner, *Mosquitoes* (New York: Boni & Liveright, 1927; New York: Pocket Books, 1985), 1. Further quotations will be given parenthetically in the text.
4. *William Faulkner: Novels 1926–1929* (New York: Library of America, 2006).
5. William Faulkner, *Sartoris* (New York: Harcourt Brace Jovanovich, 1929; Meridian, 1983), 19. Further page references will be given parenthetically in the text.
6. William Faulkner, *Flags in the Dust* (New York: Random House, 1973; Vintage, 1974), 432.
7. The "dont" in this sentence is correct as it stands. Faulkner never used apostrophes in certain words nor periods after titles like "Mr," Mrs," and "Dr". Sometimes editors changed that, and sometimes they did not.
8. William Faulkner, *The Sound and the Fury* (New York: Cape and Smith, 1929; corrected text, New York: Random House, 1984; Vintage International, 1990), 320. Further page references will be given parenthetically in the text.
9. William Faulkner, *As I Lay Dying* (New York: Cape and Smith, 1930; corrected text, New York: Random House, 1985; Vintage International, 1990), 203–4. Further page references will be given parenthetically in the text.
10. William Faulkner, *Sanctuary* (New York: Cape and Smith, 1931; corrected text, New York: Random House, Vintage International, 1993), 319–20. The editor is Noel Polk, who has produced corrected texts for all of Faulkner's novels. Further page references will be given parenthetically in the text.

11. William Faulkner, *Light in August* (New York: Smith and Haas, 1932; corrected text, New York: Random House, 1985; Vintage International, 1990), 31. Further page references will be given parenthetically in the text.

12. William Faulkner, *Pylon* (New York: Smith and Haas, 1935; corrected text, New York: Library of America, 1985; Vintage, 1987), 46. Further page references will be given parenthetically in the text.

13. William Faulkner, *Absalom, Absalom!* (New York: Random House, 1936; corrected text, New York: Random House, 1986; Vintage International, 1990), 210. Further page references will be given parenthetically in the text.

14. William Faulkner, *The Unvanquished* (New York: Random House, 1938; corrected text, New York: Library of America, 1990; Vintage International, 1991), 10. Further page references will be given parenthetically in the text.

15. William Faulkner, *If I Forget Thee, Jerusalem* (*The Wild Palms*) New York: Random House, 1939; corrected text, New York: Library of America, 1990; Vintage International, 1995), 71. Further page references will be given parenthetically in the text.

16. William Faulkner, *The Hamlet* (New York: Random House, 1940; corrected text, New York: Library of America, 1990; Vintage International, 1991), 3, 5. Further page references will be given parenthetically in the text.

17. William Faulkner, *Go Down, Moses* (New York: Random House, 1942; corrected text, New York: Random House; Vintage International, 1990), 3. Further page references will be given parenthetically in the text.

18. William Faulkner, *Intruder in the Dust* (New York: Random House, 1948; Vintage International, 1991), 3. Further page references will be given parenthetically in the text.

19. William Faulkner, *Requiem for a Nun* (New York: Random House, 1951; corrected text, *Novels 1942–1954*, New York: Library of America, 1994), 530. Further page references will be given parenthetically in the text.

20. William Faulkner, *A Fable* (New York: Random House, 1954; corrected text, *Novels 1942–1954*), 963.

21. William Faulkner, *The Town* (New York: Random House, 1957; corrected text, *Novels 1957–1962*, New York: Library of America, 1999), 2. Further page references will be given parenthetically in the text.

22. William Faulkner, *The Mansion* (New York: Random House, 1959; corrected text, *Novels 1957–1962*), 331. Further page references will be given parenthetically in the text.

23. William Faulkner, *The Reivers* (New York: Random House, 1962; corrected text, *Novels 1957–1962*), 725. Further page references will be given parenthetically in the text.

24. William Faulkner, *Collected Stories* (New York: Random House, 1950; Vintage International, 1995), 124. Further page references will be given parenthetically in the text.

3 Contexts

1. Algernon Charles Swinburne, "The Garden of Proserpine" (1866), in M. H. Abrams, ed., *The Norton Anthology of English Literature*, 2 vols. (New York: Norton, 1974), 11, 1537.
2. A. E. Housman, "To an Athlete Dying Young" (1896), *Norton Anthology of English Literature*, 2275.
3. "Clair de Lune" and "A Poplar" (1920), *William Faulkner: Early Prose and Poetry*, ed. Carvel Collins (Boston: Little, Brown, 1962), 114. Further page references will be given parenthetically in the text with the abbreviation *EPP*.
4. T. S. Eliot, "*Ulysses*, Order, and Myth," in Frank Kermode, ed., *Selected Prose of T. S. Eliot* (New York: Harvest, 1975), 177.
5. T. S. Eliot, *The Waste Land and Other Poems* (New York: Harvest, 1962), lines 19–24.
6. James Joyce, *Ulysses* (1922) (London: Penguin, 1980), 183.
7. The term "Negro" or "negro" had supplanted "colored" as the polite racial designation in 1950s America. "Black" came into favor in the 1960s and 1970s, and is still used today, along with "African American."
8. Flannery O'Connor, *Mystery and Manners: Occasional Prose* (London: Faber and Faber, 1972), 45.
9. *Conversations with Toni Morrison*, ed. Danielle Taylor Guthrie (Jackson: University Press of Mississippi, 1994), 124.

4 Critical reception

1. Granville Hicks, writing for *The Bookman* in 1931, quoted by Frederick J. Hoffman in the Introduction to Hoffman and Olga J. Vickery, eds., *William Faulkner: Three Decades of Criticism* (New York: Harbinger, 1963), 3. Further page references will be given parenthetically in the text with the abbreviation Hoffman.
2. Robert Penn Warren, ed., *Faulkner: A Collection of Critical Essays* (Englewood Cliffs, NJ: Prentice-Hall, 1966), 274. Further page references will be given parenthetically in the text with the abbreviation Warren.
3. I am indebted in this chapter to Charles A. Peek and Robert W. Hamblin, eds., *A Companion to Faulkner Studies* (Westport, CT, and London: Greenwood Press, 2004).
4. William Faulkner, *As I Lay Dying* (New York: Cape and Smith, 1930; corrected text, New York: Random House, 1985; Vintage International, 1990), 172. Further page references will be given parenthetically in the text.
5. William Faulkner, *Collected Stories* (New York: Random House, 1950; Vintage International, 1995), 895. Further page references will be given parenthetically in the text.

Guide to further reading

Primary sources: The major works by William Faulkner, including selected letters, interviews, and nonfiction, appear in the notes to Chapters 1 and 2.

Secondary sources: By no means comprehensive, this list includes works suited to a general readership rather than studies of individual texts.

Two excellent ongoing sources of information on Faulkner's works come from the University Press of Mississippi. The first is the collected essays delivered at the annual "Faulkner and Yoknapatawpha" conference at the University of Mississippi. Dedicated to a theme and separately edited, each volume appears with the subtitle *Faulkner and Yoknapatawpha*, with the year of the conference. For example, Donald M. Kartiganer and Ann J. Abadie edited *Faulkner and Gender: Faulkner and Yoknapatawpha 1994*, which appeared in 1996. The series is an excellent introduction to a broad range of accessible criticism from a number of viewpoints – highly recommended for beginning readers of Faulkner criticism. The second source from this Press is the *Reading Faulkner* series of annotations of the novels and short stories. The series explicates difficult passages and allusions and clarifies many matters for beginning and advanced readers. So far the series includes volumes on *The Sound and the Fury, Sanctuary, Light in August, The Unvanquished,* and *Collected Stories.*

Blotner, Joseph. *Faulkner: A Biography.* One-volume edition. New York: Random House, 1984. The gold standard in Faulkner biography; clearly written and informative.

Brooks, Cleanth. *William Faulkner: The Yoknapatawpha Country.* New Haven: Yale University Press, 1963. Excellent New Criticism; one of the most influential readings of the Yoknapatawpha novels.

Brown, Calvin S. *A Glossary of Faulkner's South.* New Haven and London: Yale University Press, 1976. Indispensable explanations of the fast-disappearing South that Faulkner knew.

Carothers, James B. *William Faulkner's Short Stories.* Ann Arbor: UMI Research Press, 1985. Solid New Critical reading of patterns in the short fiction.

Davis, Thadious. *Faulkner's "Negro": Art and the Southern Context.* Baton Rouge: Louisiana State University Press, 1983. With Sundquist, the starting point for modern study of race in Faulkner.

Hamblin, Robert W. and Charles A. Peek, eds. *A William Faulkner Encyclopedia.* Westport, CT: Greenwood Press, 1999. Digests of characters, works, major figures real and imagined, and intellectual movements important to Faulkner's career; highly reliable and with excellent guides to further reading.

Jehlen, Myra. *Class and Character in Faulkner's South.* New York: Columbia University Press, 1976. One of the first to apply cultural studies to Faulkner's work.

Kawin, Bruce. *Faulkner and Film.* New York: Ungar, 1977. Good guide to Faulkner and Hollywood.

Kreiswirth, Martin. *William Faulkner: The Making of a Novelist.* Athens: University of Georgia Press, 1983. Analysis of Faulkner's apprenticeship as a prose writer.

Matthews, John T. *The Play of Faulkner's Language.* Ithaca, NY: Cornell University Press, 1982. Deconstructionist reading of Faulkner's major works.

Millgate, Michael. *The Achievement of William Faulkner.* New York: Random House, 1966. Most important New Critical work on Faulkner's career, including a fine short biography.

Peek, Charles A. and Robert W. Hamblin, eds. *A Companion to Faulkner Studies.* Westport, CT: Greenwood Press, 2004. Accessible and informative essays on major schools of criticism as applied to Faulkner – mythological, postmodern, feminist, for example. Includes excellent glossary of critical terms.

Polk, Noel. *Children of the Dark House: Text and Context in Faulkner.* Jackson: University Press of Mississippi, 1996. Includes looks at Faulkner's less-known prose and performances, particularly as they reflect gender concerns.

Roberts, Diane. *Faulkner and Southern Womanhood.* Athens: University of Georgia Press, 1994. Discussion of Faulkner's use of inherited types of female characters – the lady, the mammy, for example.

Ross, Stephen M. *Fiction's Inexhaustible Voice: Speech and Writing in Faulkner.* Athens: University of Georgia Press, 1983. Insightful on auditory qualities of Faulkner's prose – a unique take.

Schwartz, Lawrence H. *Creating Faulkner's Reputation: The Politics of Modern Literary Criticism.* Knoxville: University of Tennessee Press, 1988. Reads Faulkner's career as deliberately promoted by Cold War political concerns.

Skei, Hans H. *William Faulkner: The Short Story Career.* Oslo: Universitetsforlaget, 1981. Includes useful analysis of composition and publication of the short stories.

Sundquist, Eric J. *Faulkner: The House Divided.* Baltimore and London: Johns Hopkins University Press, 1983. With Davis, the starting point for modern studies of race in Faulkner.

Towner, Theresa M. *Faulkner on the Color Line: The Later Novels.* Jackson: University Press of Mississippi, 2000. Addresses Faulkner's interest in culturally constructed ideas about "race."

Urgo, Joseph R. *Faulkner's Apocrypha: A Fable, Snopes, and the Spirit of Human Rebellion.* Jackson: University Press of Mississippi, 1989. Groundbreaking reading of Faulkner's career after 1942.

Weinstein, Philip M., ed. *The Cambridge Companion to William Faulkner.* Cambridge: Cambridge University Press, 1995. Far-ranging collection of fresh interpretations of Faulkner's career.

Williamson, Joel. *William Faulkner and Southern History.* Compendium on the topic, with the detailed biographies of Faulkner's ancestors in historical context, and the case for Colonel William Clark Falkner's "shadow family."

Index

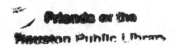